# THE BRITISH POETS,

PUBLISHED BY

## LITTLE, BROWN & COMPANY.

A COMPLETE COLLECTION,

FROM CHAUCER TO WORDSWORTH,

**Handsomely Printed in Neat 16mo. Volumes.**

**Price 75 Cents Per Volume.**

*Each Work Sold Separately.*

THIS Collection, of which more than one hundred volumes are already issued, is intended to embrace the whole works of the most distinguished authors, from Chaucer to Wordsworth, with selections from the minor poets; accompanied with biographical, historical, and critical notices and portraits, — the whole forming a far more complete, elegant, and cheap edition of the British Poets than has ever appeared before.

The numerous testimonials to the excellence of this series, which the publishers have received, both from the press and the public, in all parts of the country, would seem to indicate that a popular want has been met by this edition, which is universally acknowledged to be the best ever issued, both in point of editorship and mechanical execution.

### Notices of the Press.

"We cannot speak too highly in praise of this edition — the only one that deserves the name of 'complete' — of the British Poets." — *Boston Daily Advertiser.*

"We really know nothing more worthy of the cordial support of the American public than the Boston edition of the English poets." — *New York Times.*

"A fairer printed, a more tasteful or more valuable set of books, cannot be placed in any library." — *New York Courier and Inquirer.*

"The best, the most permanently valuable, the most convenient, and the cheapest edition of the standard poetical literature of Great Britain ever published." — *Home Journal.*

"We regard it as the most beautiful and convenient library edition of the British Poets yet published." — *Philadelphia Evening Bulletin.*

"We do not know any other edition of the English Poets which combines so much excellence." — *Bibliotheca Sacra.*

---

*The following volumes are already issued:—*

| | | | |
|---|---|---|---|
| AKENSIDE | 1 vol. | MILTON | 3 vols. |
| BALLADS | 8 vols. | MONTGOMERY | 5 " |
| BEATTIE | 1 vol. | MOORE | 6 " |
| BUTLER | 2 vols. | PARNELL & TICKELL | 1 vol. |
| CAMPBELL | 1 vol. | POPE | 3 vols. |
| CHATTERTON | 2 vols. | PRIOR | 2 " |
| CHURCHILL | 3 " | SCOTT | 9 " |
| COLERIDGE | 3 " | SHAKSPEARE | 1 vol. |
| COLLINS | 1 vol. | SHELLEY | 3 vols. |
| COWPER | 3 vols. | SKELTON | 3 " |
| DONNE | 1 vol. | SOUTHEY | 10 " |
| DRYDEN | 5 vols. | SPENSER | 5 " |
| FALCONER | 1 vol. | SURREY | 1 vol. |
| GAY | 2 vols. | SWIFT | 3 vols. |
| GOLDSMITH | 1 vol. | THOMSON | 2 " |
| GRAY | 1 " | VAUGHAN | 1 vol. |
| HERBERT | 1 " | WATTS | 1 " |
| HERRICK | 2 vols. | WHITE | 1 " |
| HOOD | 4 " | WORDSWORTH | 7 vols. |
| KEATS | 1 vol. | WYATT | 1 vol. |
| MARVELL | 1 " | YOUNG | 2 vols. |

---

*** We have in Press, and shall issue soon, the Works of

BYRON, BURNS, CHAUCER.

The remainder of the series will be published as fast as the volumes can be prepared.

# THE BRITISH ESSAYISTS,

PUBLISHED BY

## LITTLE, BROWN & COMPANY,

110 WASHINGTON STREET, BOSTON.

---

THE

## BRITISH ESSAYISTS;

WITH PREFACES, HISTORICAL AND BIOGRAPHICAL,

BY A. CHALMERS, F.S.A.

In 38 vols. 16mo.

| | | |
|---|---|---|
| Tatler, | Adventurer, | Mirror, |
| Spectator, | World, | Lounger, |
| Guardian, | Connoisseur, | Observer, |
| Rambler, | Idler, | Looker-on. |

---

The volumes are of the exact size and style of Little, Brown & Co.'s edition of the "British Poets," and sold at the same price, — seventy-five cents per volume.

The want of a neat and uniform edition of these Essays, the productions of the best writers of the English tongue, has long been felt, and the present issue is intended to supply the deficiency.

**The volumes are of convenient size, handsomely printed from the last English edition, and the price is such as to recommend them to the favor of the public, and especially of those who are engaged in making selections for school and college libraries.**

## Notices of the Press.

"These works, the flower of the best English literature for a century, merit a place in every library. They have borne a large office in the culture of mind and style for past generations, and for our elders now upon the stage; and we can wish for those entering active or literary life, access to no purer, or more copious, or more stimulating fountains of thought, sentiment, and motive, than are here." — *N. A. Review.*

"The judgment of the most competent and respected authority has been passed upon these works, and has decided that they are eminently worthy of being kept in constant use." — *Christian Examiner.*

"The value and popularity of the works included in this series will increase as those who read the English language become cultivated, and wish for compositions of the highest rank. For school and family libraries, these books are just what is needed; they are of convenient size, and attractive outward appearance, — their contents are models of composition, their spirit is liberal and manly, — their tone and influence moral and religious, without cant, or a weakness of any kind." — *Boston Transcript.*

"It is superfluous to praise the essays, — they are by general consent esteemed models of pure English style, and are full of entertainment, knowledge of the world, and moral instruction, — they will be read with pleasure as long as the English language lives." — *N. Y. Commercial Advertiser.*

"No greater service can be done in the cause of good letters than the extensive dissemination of these standard compositions. They embrace the best models of style in the English Language." — *Boston Daily Advertiser.*

"As models of English prose they stand unrivalled, and deserve a place in every library, public or private, but especially in every school and town library in the country." — *Boston Atlas.*

"A series of standard works, the value and popularity of which have only increased with time." — *N. Y. Times.*

"No more desirable edition has ever been published." — *N. Y. Evening Post.*

*Henry Kirke White –*

THE

# POETICAL WORKS

OF

# HENRY KIRKE WHITE.

WITH A MEMOIR

BY SIR HARRIS NICOLAS.

BOSTON:
LITTLE, BROWN AND COMPANY.
SHEPARD, CLARK AND BROWN.
M.DCCC.LIX.

CAMBRIDGE:
PRINTED BY ALLEN AND FARNHAM.

STEREOTYPED BY STONE AND SMART.

TO

PETER SMITH, ESQ.

THIS VOLUME

IS INSCRIBED

IN TESTIMONY OF ESTEEM AND FRIENDSHIP.

# CONTENTS.

ODES.

SONNETS.

BALLADS, SONGS, AND HYMNS.



TRIBUTARY VERSES.

# MEMOIR OF HENRY KIRKE WHITE.

BY SIR HARRIS NICOLAS.

Thine, HENRY, is a deathless name on earth,
Thine amaranthine wreaths, new pluck'd in Heaven!
By what aspiring child of mortal birth
Could more be ask'd, to whom might more be given?

TOWNSEND.

IT has been said that the contrasts of light and shade are as necessary to biography as to painting, and that the character which is radiant with genius and virtue requires to be relieved by more common and opposite qualities. Though this may be true as a principle, there are many exceptions; and the life of HENRY KIRKE WHITE, whose merits were unalloyed by a single vice, is one of the most memorable. The history of his short and melancholy career, by Mr. Southey, is extremely popular; and when it is remembered that its author is one of the most distinguished of living writers, that as a biographer he is unrivalled, and that he had access to all the materials which exist, it would be as vain to expect from the present Memoir any new facts, as it would be absurd to hope that it will be more worthy of attention than the imperishable monument which his generous friend has erected to his memory.

There is, however, nothing inconsistent with this admission, in presuming that a Life of the Poet might be written almost as interesting as the one alluded to, and without the writer assuming to himself any unusual sagacity. As Mr. Southey's narrative is prefixed to a collection of all Kirke White's remains, in prose as well as in verse, his letters are inserted as part of his works, instead of extracts from them being introduced into the Memoir. This volume will, on the contrary, be confined to his Poems; and such parts of his letters as describe his situation and feelings at particular periods will be introduced into the account of his life. Indeed, so frequent are the allusions to himself in those letters as well as in his poems, that he may be almost considered an autobiographer; and the writer who substitutes his own cold and lifeless sketch for the glowing and animated portrait which these memorials of genius afford, must either be deficient in skill, or be under the dominion of overweening vanity.

Few who have risen to eminence were, on the paternal side at least, of humbler origin than HENRY KIRKE WHITE. His father, John White, was a butcher at Nottingham; but his mother, who bore the illustrious name of Neville, is said to have belonged to a respectable family in Staffordshire.

He was born at Nottingham on the 21st of March, 1785; and in his earliest years indications were observed of the genius for which he was afterwards distinguished. In his poem "Childhood," he has graphically described the little school where, between the age of three and five, he

> "enter'd, though with toil and pain,
> The low vestibule of learning's fane."

The venerable dame by whom he was

> "inured to alphabetic toils,"

and whose worth he gratefully commemorates, had the discernment to perceive her charge's talents, and even foretold his future celebrity:

> "And, as she gave my diligence its praise,
> Talk'd of the honour of my future days."

If he did not deceive himself, it was at this period that his imagination became susceptible of poetic associations. Speaking of the eagerness with which he left the usual sports of children to listen to tales of imaginary woe, and of the effect which they produced, he says,

> "Beloved moment! then 't was first I caught
> The first foundation of romantic thought;
> Then first I shed bold Fancy's thrilling tear,
> Then first that Poesy charm'd mine infant ear.
> Soon stored with much of legendary lore,
> The sports of childhood charm'd my soul no more;
> Far from the scene of gaiety and noise,
> Far, far from turbulent and empty joys,

I hied me to the thick o'erarching shade,
And there, on mossy carpet, listless laid;
While at my feet the rippling runnel ran,
The days of wild romance antique I'd scan;
Soar on the wings of fancy through the air,
To realms of light, and pierce the radiance there."

The peculiar disposition of his mind, having thus early displayed itself, every day added to its force. Study and abstraction were his greatest pleasures, and a love of reading became his predominant passion. "I could fancy," said his eldest sister, "I see him in his little chair with a large book upon his knee, and my mother calling, 'Henry, my love, come to dinner,' which was repeated so often without being regarded, that she was obliged to change the tone of her voice before she could rouse him."

At the age of six he was placed under the care of the Rev. John Blanchard, who kept the best school in Nottingham, where he learnt writing, arithmetic, and French; and he continued there for several years. During that time two facts are related of him which prove the precocity of his talents. When about seven, he was accustomed to go secretly into his father's kitchen and teach the servant to read and write; and he composed a tale of a Swiss emigrant, which he gave her, being too diffident to show it to his mother. In his eleventh year he wrote a separate theme for each of the twelve or fourteen boys in his class; and the excellence of the various pieces obtained his master's applause.

Henry was destined for his father's trade, and the efforts of his mother to change that intention were for some time fruitless. Even while he was at school, one day in every week, and his leisure hours on the others, were employed in carrying meat to his father's customers; but a dispute between his father and his master having caused him to be removed from school, one of the ushers, from malice or ignorance, told his mother that it was impossible to make her son do any thing. The person who reported so unfavourably of his abilities, little knew that he had then given ample evidence of his talents, in some poetical satires which his treatment at school had provoked, but which he afterwards destroyed.

Soon after he quitted Mr. Blanchard's school he was intrusted to Mr. Shipley, who discovered his pupil's abilities, and relieved his friends' uneasiness on the subject. His earliest production that has been preserved was written in his thirteenth year, "On being confined to School one pleasant Morning in Spring," in which a schoolboy's love of liberty, and his envy of the freedom of a neighbouring wren, are expressed with plaintive simplicity.

About this time a slight improvement took place in his situation. His mother, to whom he was indebted for all the happiness of his childhood, opened a day school, and, as it abstracted her from the groveling cares of a butcher's shop, his home was made much more comfortable; and, instead of being confined to his father's business, he was placed in a stocking loom, with the view of bringing him up to the trade of a hosier, the poverty of his family still precluding the hope of a profession.

It may easily be believed that this occupation ill agreed with the aspirations of his mind. From his mother he had few secrets, and in her ear he breathed his disgust and unhappiness. "He could not bear," he said, "the idea of spending some years of his life in shining and folding up stockings;" he wanted "something to occupy his brain, and he should be wretched if he continued longer at this trade, or indeed in any thing, except one of the learned professions." For a year these remonstrances were ineffectual; but no persuasions, even when urged with maternal tenderness, could reconcile him to his lot. He sought for consolation with the Muses, and wrote an "Address to Contemplation," in which he describes his feelings:

"Why along
The dusky track of commerce should I toil,
When, with an easy competence content,
I can alone be happy; where, with thee,
I may enjoy the loveliness of Nature,
And loose the wings of fancy! Thus alone
Can I partake of happiness on earth;
And to be happy here is man's chief end,
For to be happy he must needs be good."

There are few obstacles that perseverance will not overcome; and penury and a parent's obstinacy were both surmounted by Kirke White's importunity. Finding it useless to chain him longer to the hosier's loom, he was placed in the office of Messrs. Coldham and Enfield, Town Clerk and attorneys of Nottingham, some time in May, 1799, when he was in his fifteenth year; but as a premium could not be given with him, it was agreed that he should serve two years before he was articled. A few months after he entered upon his new employment, he began a correspondence with his brother, Mr. Neville White, who was then a medical student in London; and in a letter, dated in September, 1799, he thus spoke of his situation and prospects:

"It is now nearly four months since I entered into Mr. Coldham's office; and it is with pleasure I can assure you, that I never yet found any thing disagreeable, but, on the contrary, every thing I do seems a pleasure to me, and for a very obvious reason, — it is a business which I like — a business which I chose before all others; and I have two good-tempered, easy masters, but who will, nevertheless, see that their business is done in a neat and proper manner." — "A man that understands the law is sure to have business; and in case I have no thoughts, in case, that is, that I do not aspire to hold the honourable place of a barrister, I shall feel sure of gaining a genteel livelihood at the business to which I am articled."

At the suggestion of his employers, he devoted the greater part of his leisure to Latin; and, though he was but slightly assisted, he was able in ten months to read Horace with tolerable facility, and had made some progress in Greek. Having but little time for these pursuits, he accustomed himself to decline the Greek nouns and verbs during his walks to and from the office, and he thereby acquired a habit of studying while walking, that never deserted him. The account which Mr. Southey has given of his application, and of the success that attended it, is astonishing. Though living with his family, he nearly estranged himself from their society. At meals, and during the evenings, a book was constantly in his hands; and as he refused to sup with them, to prevent any loss of time, his meal was sent to him in his little apartment. Law, Greek, Latin, Italian, Spanish, and Portuguese, chemistry, astronomy, electricity, drawing, music, and mechanics, by turns engaged his attention; and though his acquirements in some of those studies were very superficial, his proficiency in many of them was far from contemptible. His papers on law evince so much industry, that had that subject alone occupied his leisure hours, his diligence would have been commendable. He was a tolerable Italian scholar, and in the classics he afterwards attained reputation; but of the sciences and of Spanish and Portuguese, his knowledge was not, it may be inferred, very great. His ear for music was good, and his passionate attachment to it is placed beyond a doubt by his verses on its effects:

> "With her in pensive mood I long to roam
> At midnight's hour, or evening's calm decline,
> And thoughtful o'er the falling streamlet's foam,
> In calm Seclusion's hermit-walks recline:"

But he checked his ardour, lest it might interfere with more essential studies: and his musical attainments were limited to playing pleasingly on the piano, composing the bass to the air at the same time.

Ambition was one of the most powerful feelings of his nature, and it is rare indeed, when it is not the companion of great talents. It developed itself first in spurning trade; and no sooner did he find himself likely to become an attorney, than he aspired to the bar. But his earliest and strongest passion was for literary distinction; and he was scarcely removed from the trammels of school, before he sought admission into a literary society, in his native town. His extreme youth rendered him objectionable; but, after repeated refusals, he at last succeeded. In the association there were six professors, and being, on the first vacancy, appointed to the chair of literature, he soon justified the choice. Taking "genius" as his theme, he addressed the assembly in an extemporaneous lecture of two hours and three-quarters duration, with so much success, that the audience unanimously voted him their thanks, declaring that "the society had never heard a better lecture delivered from the chair which he so much honoured." To judge properly of this circumstance, it would be necessary to know of whom the society was composed; but with so flattering a testimony to his abilities, the sanguine boy naturally placed a high estimate on them.

The establishment of a Magazine called the Monthly Preceptor, which proposed prize themes for young persons, afforded Kirke White an opportunity of trying his literary powers. In a letter written in June, 1800, to his brother, speaking of that work he says, "I am noticed as worthy of commendation, and as affording an encouraging prospect of future excellence. You will laugh. I have also turned poet, and have translated an Ode of Horace into English verse." His productions gained him several of the prizes; and he soon afterwards became a contributor to the Monthly Mirror, his compositions in which attracted the attention of Mr. Hill, the proprietor of the work, and of Mr. Capel Lofft, a gentleman who distinguished himself by his patronage of Bloomfield.

Though on entering an attorney's office the bar was the object of his hopes, a constitutional deafness soon convinced him that he was not adapted for the duties of an advocate; and his thoughts, from conscientious motives, became directed to the Church.

When about fifteen, his mind was agitated by doubt and anxiety on the most important of all subjects; and the chaos of opinions which extensive and miscellaneous reading so often produces on ardent and imaginative temperaments, is well described in his little poem entitled, "My own Character," wherein he represents himself as a prey to the most opposite impressions, and as being in a miserable state of incertitude:

> " First I premise it's my honest conviction,
> That my breast is the chaos of all contradiction,
> Religious — deistic — now loyal and warm,
> Then a dagger-drawn democrat hot for reform;
> . . . . . . . . . . . . . . .
> Now moody and sad, now unthinking and gay,
> To all points of the compass I veer in a day."

In this sketch there is evidently much truth; and it affords a striking idea of a plastic and active mind, on which every thing makes an impression, where one idea follows another in such rapid succession, that the former is not so entirely removed, but that some remains of it are amalgamated with its successor. A youth whose intellect is thus tossed in a whirlpool of conflicting speculations, resembles a goodly ship newly launched, which, until properly steadied by ballast, reels from side to side, the sport of every undulation of the waters.

About this time young White's religious feelings were strongly affected by the conversion of his friend, Mr. Almond, whose opinions were previously as unsettled as his own. To escape the raillery with which he expected White would assail him on learning the change in his sentiments, Almond avoided his society; and when his friend offered to defend his opinions, if Henry would allow the divine originality of the Bible, he exclaimed, "Good God! you surely regard me in a worse light than I deserve." The discussion that followed, and the perusal of Scott's "Force of Truth," which Almond placed in his hands, induced him to direct his attention seriously to the subject; but an affecting incident soon afterwards showed how deeply he was then influenced by religious considerations. On the evening before Mr. Almond left Nottingham for Cambridge, he was requested by White to accompany him to his apartment. The moment they entered, Henry burst into tears, declaring that his anguish of mind was insupportable; and he entreated Almond to kneel and pray for him. Their tears and supplications were cordially mingled, and when they were about to separate, White said, "What must I do? You are the only friend to whom I can apply in this agonizing state, and you are about to leave me. My literary associates are all inclined to deism. I have no one with whom I can communicate."

It is instructive to learn to what circumstance such a person as Kirke White was indebted for the knowledge "which causes not to err." This information occurs in a letter from him to a Mr. Booth, in August, 1801; and it also fixes the date of the happy change that influenced every thought and every action of his future life, which gave the energy of virtue to his exertions, soothed the asperities of a temper naturally impetuous and irritable, and enabled him, at a period when manhood is full of hope and promise, to view the approaches of death with the calmness of a philosopher, and the resignation of a saint.

After thanking Mr. Booth for the present of Jones's work on the Trinity, he thus describes his religious impressions previous to its perusal, and the effect it produced:

"Religious polemics, indeed, have seldom formed a part of my studies; though whenever I happened accidentally to turn my thoughts to the subject of the Protestant doctrine of the Godhead, and compared it with Arian and Socinian, many doubts interfered, and I even began to think that the more nicely the subject was investigated, the more perplexed it would appear, and was on the point of forming a resolution to go to heaven in my own way, without meddling or involving myself in the inextricable labyrinth of controversial dispute, when I received and perused this excellent treatise, which finally cleared up the mists which my ignorance had conjured around me, and clearly pointed out the real truth."

From the moment he became convinced of the truths of Christianity, all the enthusiasm of his nature was kindled. The ministry only, was deemed worthy of his ambition; and he devoted his thoughts to the sacred office with a zeal that justified a hope of the richest fruits. In a letter to his friend, Mr. Almond, in November, 1803, he says,

"My dear friend, I cannot adequately express

what I owe to you on the score of religion. I told Mr. Robinson you were the first instrument of my being brought to think deeply on religious subjects; and I feel more and more every day, that if it had not been for you, I might, most probably, have been now buried in apathy and unconcern. Though I am in a great measure blessed,—I mean blessed with faith, now pretty steadfast, and heavy convictions, I am far from being happy. My sins have been of a dark hue, and manifold: I have made Fame my God, and Ambition my shrine. I have placed all my hopes on the things of this world. I have knelt to Dagon; I have worshipped the evil creations of my own proud heart, and God had well nigh turned his countenance from me in wrath; perhaps one step further, and he might have shut me for ever from his rest. I now turn my eyes to Jesus, my Saviour, my atonement, with hope and confidence: he will not repulse the imploring penitent; his arms are open to all, they are open even to me; and in return for such a mercy, what can I do less than dedicate my whole life to his service? My thoughts would fain recur at intervals to my former delights; but I am now on my guard to restrain and keep them in. I know now where they ought to concentre, and with the blessing of God, they shall there all tend.

"My next publication of poems will be solely religious. I shall not destroy those of a different nature, which now lie before me; but they will, most probably, sleep in my desk, until, in the good time of my great Lord and Master, I shall receive my passport from this world of vanity. I am now bent on a higher errand than that of the attainment of poetical fame; poetry, in future, will be my relaxation, not my employment.—Adieu to literary ambition! 'You do not aspire to be prime minister,' said Mr. Robinson; 'you covet a far higher character—to be the humblest among those who minister to their Maker.'"

To the arguments of his friends on the impolicy of quitting a profession to which he had given so much of his time, and on the obstacles to the attainment of his wishes, he was impenetrable. His employers generously offered to cancel his articles as soon as he could show that his resources were likely to support him at the University. Friends arose as they became necessary, and more than one or two persons exerted themselves to promote his views; but his principal reliance was on the sale of a little volume of Poems, which, at the suggestion of Mr. Capel Lofft, he prepared for the press.

The history of an author's first book is always interesting, and Kirke White's was attended with unusual incidents. A novice in literature often imagines that it is important his work should be dedicated to some person of rank; and the Countess of Derby was applied to, who declined, on the ground that she never accepted a compliment of that nature. He then addressed the Duchess of

Devonshire; and a letter, with the manuscript, was left at her house. The difficulty of obtaining access to her Grace proved so great, that more than one letter to his brother was written on the subject, in which he indignantly says, "I am cured of patronage hunting; as for begging patronage, I am tired to the soul of it, and shall give it up." Permission to inscribe the book to the Duchess was at length granted: the book came out in 1803; and a copy was transmitted to her, of which, however, no notice whatever was taken.

On the publication of the volume, a copy was sent to each Review, with a letter deprecatory of the severity of criticism, an act as ill judged as it was useless, since all that a young writer could properly say was to be found in the preface, in which he stated that his inducement to publish was, "the facilitation through its means of those studies which, from his earliest infancy, have been the principal objects of his ambition, and the increase of the capacity to pursue these inclinations, which may one day place him in an honourable station in the scale of society."

His feelings received a severe wound from the notice of his Poems in the Monthly Review, the writer of which, not satisfied with saying that the production did not "justify any sanguine expectations," selected four of the worst lines in support of his opinion, and showed himself insensible of the numerous beauties scattered through the various pieces. Writing to a friend soon afterwards, he thus spoke of himself; and more mental wretchedness has seldom been described:

"I am at present under afflictions and contentions of spirit, heavier than I have yet ever experienced. I think, at times, I am mad, and destitute of religion; my pride is not yet subdued: the unfavourable review (in the 'Monthly') of my unhappy work, has cut deeper than you could have thought; not in a literary point of view, but as it affects my respectability. It represents me actually as a beggar, going about gathering money to put myself at college, when my book is worthless; and this with every appearance of candour. They have been sadly misinformed respecting me: this review goes before me wherever I turn my steps; it haunts me incessantly, and I am persuaded it is an instrument in the hand of Satan to drive me to distraction. I must leave Nottingham. If the answer of the Elland Society be unfavourable, I purpose writing to the Marquis of Wellesley, to offer myself as a student at the academy he has instituted at Fort William, in Bengal, and at the proper age to take orders there. The missionaries at that place have done wonders already; and I should, I hope, be a valuable labourer in the vineyard. If the Marquis take no notice of my application, or do not accede to my proposal, I shall place myself in some other way of making a meet preparation for the holy office, either in the Calvinistic Academy, or in one of the Scotch Universities, where I shall be able to live at scarcely any expense."

The criticism just adverted to was as unfeeling as unjust; and but for the generous conduct of a distinguished living poet, whose benevolence of heart is equal to his genius, it might have entirely crushed his hopes. Disgusted at the injustice of this criticism, Mr. Southey instantly wrote to White, expressing his opinion of the merits of his book, and giving him the encouragement and advice which none was ever more ready or more able to bestow. Thus, an act of cruel folly proved in its consequences the most beneficial of the Poet's life. His spirits were invigorated by this considerate kindness, and his feelings were expressed in glowing terms:

"I dare not say all I feel respecting your opinion of my little volume. The extreme acrimony with which the Monthly Review (of all others the most important) treated me, threw me into a state of stupefaction. I regarded all that had passed as a dream, and I thought I had been deluding myself into an idea of possessing poetic genius, when, in fact, I had only the longing, without the *afflatus*. I mustered resolution enough, however, to write spiritedly to them: their answer, in the ensuing number, was a tacit acknowledgment that they had been somewhat too unsparing in their correction. It was a poor attempt to salve over a wound wantonly and most ungenerously inflicted. Still I was damped, because I knew the work was very respectable; and therefore could not, I concluded, give a criticism grossly deficient in equity, the more especially, as I knew of no sort of inducement to extraordinary severity. Your letter, however, has revived me, and I do again venture to hope that I may still produce something which will survive me. With regard to your advice and offers of assistance, I will not attempt, because I am unable, to thank you for them. To-morrow morning I depart for Cambridge; and I have considerable hopes that, as I do not enter into the University with any sinister or interested views, but sincerely desire to perform the duties of an affectionate and vigilant pastor, and become more useful to mankind; I therefore have hopes, I say, that I shall find means of support in the University. If I do not, I shall certainly act in pursuance of your recommendations; and shall, without hesitation, avail myself of your offers of service, and of your directions. In a short time this will be determined; and when it is, I shall take the liberty of writing to you at Keswick, to make you acquainted with the result. I have only one objection to publishing by subscription, and I confess it has weight with me; it is, that, in this step, I shall seem to be acting upon the advice so unfeelingly and contumeliously given by the Monthly Reviewers, who say what is equal to this, that had I gotten a subscription for my poems before their merit was known, I might have succeeded; provided, it seems, I had made a particular statement of my case; like a beggar who stands with his hat in one hand, and a full account of his cruel treatment on the coast of Barbary in the other, and so gives you his penny sheet for your sixpence, by way of half purchase, half charity. I have materials for another volume; but they were written principally while Clifton Grove was in the press, or soon after, and do not now at all satisfy me. Indeed, of late, I have been obliged to desist, almost entirely, from converse with the dames of Helicon. The drudgery of an attorney's office, and the necessity of preparing myself, in case I should succeed in getting to college, in what little leisure I could boast, left no room for the flights of the imagination."

As soon as there were reasonable hopes of an adequate support being obtained for him at Cambridge, he went to the village of Wilford, for a month, to recruit his health, on which intense application had made great inroads. Near this place were Clifton Woods, the subject of one of his Poems, and which had long been his favourite resort. Here he fully indulged in that love of the beauties of nature, which forms a leading trait in the Poetic character: and on this occasion he gave full reins to those reveries of the imagination, of the delight of which a Poet only is sensible. His lines on Wilford Church Yard show the melancholy tone of his mind; and those Verses, as well as his "Ode to Disappointment," of which no praise would be too extravagant, appear to have been written, on learning from his mother, before he left Wilford, that the efforts made to place him at Cambridge had failed. It was evidently to this circumstance, which for the time blighted his aspirations, that he alluded, when he says he was,

"From Hope's summit hurl'd."

His remark to his mother on this occasion evinced, nevertheless, great energy of mind. His complaints were confined to verse, for the disappointment had no other effect upon his conduct than to induce him to apply to his studies with unprecedented vigour, that, since he was to revert to the law as a profession, he might not be, as he observed, "a *mediocre* attorney." He read regularly from five in the morning until some time after midnight, and occasionally passed whole nights without lying down; and the entreaties, even when accompanied by the tears of his mother, that he would not thus destroy his health, did not induce him to relax his zeal.

Symptoms of consumption, the disease to which he ultimately became a victim, and which he designates, in one of his many allusions to it, as

"The most fatal of Pandora's train,"

began now to excite the anxiety of his family. Illness was, however, forgotten in the realization of the hope dearest to his heart. The exertions of his friends proved successful at a time when all expectations had vanished; and by their united efforts it was resolved that he should become a sizer of St. John's College, Cambridge, his brother Neville, his mother, and a benevolent individual, whose name is not mentioned, having agreed to contribute to support him. It appears, that if he had not succeeded in that object, he intended to have joined the society of orthodox dissenters, for which purpose he underwent an examination. Though his attainments and character proved satisfactory on that occasion, his volume of Poems rose in judgment against him, and nothing but the approbation Mr. Southey had expressed of them prevented his work from being considered a disqualification for the ministry. His feelings on the prospect of entering the Church are described with great force in his letter, dated in April, 1804.

"Most fervently do I return thanks to God for this providential opening: it has breathed new animation into me, and my breast expands with the prospect of becoming the minister of Christ where I most desired it; but where I almost feared all probability of success was nearly at an end. Indeed, I had begun to turn my thoughts to the dissenters, as people of whom I was destined, not by choice, but necessity, to become the pastor. Still, although I knew I should be happy anywhere, so that I were a profitable labourer in the vineyard, I did, by no means, feel that calm, that indescribable satisfaction which I do when I look toward that

Church, which I think in the main formed on the apostolic model, and from which I am decidedly of opinion there is no positive grounds for dissent. I return thanks to God for keeping me so long in suspense, for I know it has been beneficial to my soul, and I feel a considerable trust that the way is now about to be made clear, and that my doubts and fears on this head will, in due time, be removed."

Being advised to degrade for a year, and to place himself with a private tutor, he went to the Rev. Mr. Grainger of Winteringham, in Lincolnshire, in the autumn of 1804. While under that gentleman's care he studied with such intense fervour, that fears were excited not for his health only, but for his intellect; and a second severe attack of illness was the consequence. Poetry was now laid aside, and as he himself told a friend in February, 1805,

"My poor neglected Muse has lain absolutely unnoticed by me for the last four months, during which period I have been digging in the mines of Scapula for Greek roots, and instead of drinking with eager delight the beauties of Virgil have been culling and drying his phrases for future use." — "I fear my good genius, who was wont to visit me with nightly visions in woods and brakes and by the river's marge, is now dying of a fen ague, and I shall thus probably emerge from my retreat not a hair-brained son of imagination, but a sedate black-lettered book worm, with a head like an etymologicon magnum."

To Mr. Capel Lofft, in the September following, after stating that all his time was employed in preparing himself for orders, his estimate of the necessary qualifications being very high, he observed:

"I often, however, cast a look of fond regret to the darling occupations of my younger hours, and the tears rush into my eyes, as I fancy I see the few wild flowers of poetic genius, with which I have been blessed, withering with neglect. Poetry has been to me something more than amusement; it has been a cheering companion when I have had no other to fly to, and a delightful solace when consolation has been in some measure needful. I cannot, therefore, discard so old and faithful a friend without deep regret, especially when I reflect that, stung by my ingratitude, he may desert me for ever!"

But the old fire was, he adds, rekindled by looking over some of his pieces which Mr. Lofft wished to print; and he transmitted to that gentleman a short Poem, expressive of his sorrow at taking leave of his favourite pursuit. The following passages could only have arisen from a love of Poetry, which it was not in the power of severer studies to extinguish:

Heart-soothing Poesy! Though thou hast ceased
To hover o'er the many voiced strings
Of my long silent lyre, yet thou canst still
Call the warm tear from its thrice hallow'd cell,

And with recalled images of bliss
Warm my reluctant heart. Yes, I would throw,
Once more would throw, a quick and hurried hand
O'er the responding chords. It hath not ceased,
It cannot, will not cease; the heavenly warmth
Plays round my heart, and mantles o'er my cheek;
Still, though unbidden, plays. Fair Poesy!
The summer and the spring, the wind and rain,
Sunshine and storm, with various interchange,
Have mark'd full many a day, and week, and month,
Since by dark wood, or hamlet far retired,
Spell-struck, with thee I loiter'd. Sorceress!
I cannot burst thy bonds!

In October, 1805, Kirke White became a resident member of St. John's College, Cambridge; and such was the use he had made of his time at Winteringham, that he was distinguished for his classical knowledge. But he had dearly purchased his superiority. His constitution was much shattered when he went to Mr. Grainger, and every day brought with it new proofs that his career had nearly reached its bounds. The only chance of prolonging his life was to seek a milder climate, and to abandon study entirely. As in all great minds, Fame was, however, dearer to him than existence. He felt that every thing connected with his future prospects was at stake; and he adhered to a course of rigorous application until nature gave way. During his first term he became a candidate for one of the University scholarships; but the increased exertion he underwent was attended by results that obliged him to retire from the contest. At this moment the general college examination approached, and thinking that if he failed his hopes would be blasted for ever, he taxed his energies to the uttermost, during the fortnight which intervened, to meet the trial. His illness, however, speedily returned; and, with tears in his eyes, he informed his tutor, Mr. Catton, that he could not go into the Hall to be examined. That gentleman, whose kindness to the Poet entitles his name to respect, urged him to support himself during the six days of the examination. Powerful stimulants were administered, and he was pronounced the first man of his year. The triumph, complete and exhilarating as it was, too closely resembled that of the generous steed, who, in distancing his competitors, reaches the goal, and dies; and his own ideas of the sacrifices with which such an honour must be attended were very poetical. He said to an intimate friend, almost the last time he saw him, that were he to paint a picture of Fame crowning a distinguished under graduate after the senate house examination, he would represent her as concealing a death's head under a mask of beauty.

Soon after this event, Kirke White went to London, and on Christmas Eve he wrote to his mother from town, stating that his health had been rather affected by study, that he came to London for amusement, and that his tutor had, in the kindest manner, relieved his mind from pecuniary cares, and cheered him with the assurance that his talents would be rewarded by his College. But it is from his letters to his friend that the real state to which excitement and labour had reduced him, is to be learnt, because, to allay the fears of his relations, he represented himself to them, as being much better than he actually was:

London, Christmas, 1805.

"I wrote you a letter, which now lies in my drawer at St. John's; but in such a weak state of body, and in so desponding and comfortless a tone of mind, that I knew it would give you pain, and therefore I chose not to send it. I have indeed been ill; but thanks to God, I am recovered. My nerves were miserably shattered by over application, and the absence of all that could amuse, and the presence of many things which weighed heavy upon my spirits. When I found myself too ill to read, and too desponding to endure my own reflections, I discovered that it is really a miserable thing to be destitute of the soothing and supporting hand when nature most needs it. I wandered up and down from one man's room to another, and from one College to another, imploring society, a little conversation, and a little relief of the burden which pressed upon my spirits; and I am sorry to say, that those who, when I was cheerful and lively, sought my society with avidity, now, when I actually needed conversation, were too busy to grant it. Our College examination was then approaching, and I perceived with anguish that I had read for the university scholarship until I had barely time to get up our private subjects, and that as I was now too ill to read, all hope of getting through the examination with decent respectability was at an end. This was an additional grief. I went to our tutor, with tears in my eyes, and told him I must absent myself from the examination, — a step which would have precluded me from a station amongst the prize-men until the second year. He earnestly entreated me to run the risk. My surgeon gave me strong stimulants and supporting medicines during the examination week; and I passed, I believe, one of the most respectable examinations amongst them. As soon as ever it was over, I left Cambridge, by the advice of my surgeon and tutor, and I feel myself now pretty strong. I have given up the thought of sitting for the University scholarship, in consequence of my illness, as the course of my reading was effectually broken. In this place I have been much amused, and have been received with an attention in the literary circles which I neither expected nor deserved. But this does not affect me as it once would have done: my views are widely altered; and I hope that I shall in time learn to lay my whole heart at the foot of the cross."

Early in January following he returned to Cambridge, and imprudently resumed his old habits of study, according to the following plan: "Rise at half-past five; devotions and walk till seven; chapel and breakfast till eight; study and lectures till one; four and a half clear reading; walk, &c. and dinner, and Wollaston, and chapel to six; six to nine reading, three hours; nine to ten devotions; bed at ten." With him, however, exercise was but slight relaxation, as his intellectual faculties were kept on the stretch during his walks, and he is known to have committed to memory a whole tragedy of Euripides in this manner, and as they were not less exerted in his devotions, his mind must have been intensely occupied for twelve or fourteen hours a day, at a moment when perfect quiet and rest were indispensable. Within a very few weeks he paid a heavy penalty for his indiscretion. To his friend, Mr. Maddock, he wrote on the 17th of February, 1806:

"Do not think I am reading hard; I believe it is all over with that. I have had a recurrence of my old complaint within this last four or five days, which has half unnerved me for every thing. The state of my health is really miserable; I am well and lively in the morning, and overwhelmed with nervous horrors in the evening. I do not know how to proceed with regard to my studies: — a very slight overstretch of the mind in the daytime occasions me not only a sleepless night, but a night of gloom and horror. The systole and diastole of my heart seem to be playing at ball — the stake, my life. I can only say the game is not yet decided: — I allude to the violence of the palpitation. I am going to mount the Gog-magog hills this morning, in quest of a good night's sleep. The Gog-magog hills for my body, and the Bible for my mind, are my only medicines. I am sorry to say, that neither are quite adequate. Cui, igitur; dandum est vitio? Mihi prorsus. I hope, as the summer comes, my spirits (which have been with the swallows, a winter's journey) will come with it. When my spirits are restored, my health will be restored: — the 'fons mali' lies there. Give me serenity and equability of mind, and all will be well."

He, however, rallied again; but he seems to have been aware that his end was not far distant, for in March he told his brother that though his stay at Cambridge, in the long vacation, was important, he intended to go to Nottingham for his health, and more particularly for his mother's sake; adding, "I shall be glad to moor all my family in the harbour of religious trust, and in the calm seas of religious peace. These concerns are apt at times to escape me; but they now press much upon my heart, and I think it is my first duty to see that my family are safe in the most important of all affairs."

In April, however, he drew a pleasing picture of his future life, in which his filial and paternal tenderness are conspicuous; but he soon afterwards went to Nottingham; and in a letter to his friend Mr. Leeson, written from that town, on the 7th of April, he gave a very melancholy account of himself:

"It seems determined upon, by my mother, that I cannot be spared, since the time of my stay is so very short, and my health so very uncertain. The people here can scarcely be persuaded that any thing ails me; so well do I look; but occasional depressions, especially after any thing has occurred to occasion uneasiness, still harass me. My mind is of a very peculiar cast. I began to think too early; and the indulgence of certain trains of thought, and too free an exercise of the imagination, have superinduced a morbid kind of sensibility; which is to the mind what excessive irritability is to the body. Some circumstances occurred on my arrival at Nottingham, which gave me just cause for inquietude and anxiety; the consequences were insomnia, and a relapse into causeless dejections. It is my business now to curb these irrational and immoderate affections, and, by accustoming myself to sober thought and cool reasoning, to restrain these freaks and vagaries of the fancy, and redundancies of μελαγχολια. When I am well, I cannot help entertaining a sort of contempt for the weakness of mind which marks my indispositions. Titus when well, and Titus when ill, are two distinct persons. The man, when in health, despises the man, when ill, for his weakness, and the latter envies the former for his felicity."

As his health declined his prospects seemed to brighten. He was again pronounced first at the great College examination; he was one of the three best theme writers, whose merits were so nearly equal that the examiners could not decide between them; and he was a prize-man both in the mathematical and logical or general examination, and in Latin composition. His College offered him a private tutor at its expense, and Mr. Catton obtained exhibitions for him to the value of sixty-six pounds per annum, by which he was enabled to give up the pecuniary assistance he had received from his friends. But even at this moment, when the world promised so much, his situation was truly deplorable. The highest honours of the University were supposed to be within his grasp, and the conviction that such was the general opinion, goaded him on to the most strenuous exertions when he was incapable of the slightest. This struggle between his mental and physical powers, was not, however, of long duration. In July he was seized with an attack that threatened his life, and which he thus described in a letter to Mr. Maddock:

"Last Saturday morning I rose early, and got

up some rather abstruse problems in mechanics for my tutor, spent an hour with him, between eight and nine got my breakfast, and read the Greek History (at breakfast) till ten, then sat down to decipher some logarithm tables. I think I had not done any thing at them, when I lost myself. At a quarter past eleven my laundress found me bleeding in four different places in my face and head, and insensible. I got up and staggered about the room, and she, being frightened, ran away, and told my gyp to fetch a surgeon. Before he came I was sallying out with my flannel gown on, and my academical gown over it; he made me put on my coat, and then I went to Mr. Farish's: he opened a vein, and my recollection returned. My own idea was, that I had fallen out of bed, and so I told Mr. Farish at first; but I afterwards remembered that I had been to Mr. Fiske, and breakfasted. Mr. Catton has insisted on my consulting Sir Isaac Pennington, and the consequence is, that I am to go through a course of blistering, &c. which, after the bleeding, will leave me weak enough.

"I am, however, very well, except as regards the doctors, and yesterday I drove into the country to Saffron Walden, in a gig. My tongue is in a bad condition, from a bite which I gave it either in my fall, or in the moments of convulsion. My nose has also come badly off. I believe I fell against my reading desk. My other wounds are only rubs and scratches on the carpet. I am ordered to remit my studies for a while, by the common advice both of doctors and tutors. Dr. Pennington hopes to prevent any recurrence of the fit. He thinks it looks towards epilepsy, of the horrors of which malady I have a very full and precise idea; and I only pray that God will spare me as respects my faculties, however else it may seem good to him to afflict me. Were I my own master, I know how I should act; but I am tied here by bands which I cannot burst. I know that change of place is needful; but I must not indulge in the idea. The college must not pay my tutor for nothing. Dr. Pennington and Mr. Farish attribute the attack to a too continued tension of the faculties. As I am much alone now, I never get quite off study, and I think incessantly. I know nature will not endure this. They both proposed my going home, but Mr. * * did not hint at it, although much concerned; and, indeed, I know home would be a bad place for me in my present situation. I look round for a resting place, and I find none. Yet there is one, which I have long too, too much disregarded, and thither I must now betake myself. There are many situations worse than mine, and I have no business to complain. If these afflictions should draw the bonds tighter which hold me to my Redeemer, it will be well. You may be assured that you have here a plain statement of my case in its true colours without any palliation. I am now well again, and have only to fear a relapse, which I shall do all I can to prevent, by a relaxation in study. I have now written too much.

"I am, very sincerely yours,

"H. K. WHITE.

"P. S. I charge you, as you value my peace, not to let my friends hear, either directly or indirectly of my illness."

A few weeks afterwards he again directed his mother's hopes to a tranquil retreat for his family in his parsonage, but said nothing of his illness; and he told Mr. Maddock, in September,

"I am perfectly well again, and have experienced no recurrence of the fit: my spirits, too, are better, and I read very moderately. I hope that God will be pleased to spare his rebellious child; this stroke has brought me nearer to Him; whom indeed have I for my comforter but Him? I am still reading, but with moderation, as I have been during the whole vacation, whatever you may persist in thinking. My heart turns with more fondness towards the consolations of religion than it did, and in some degree I have found consolation."

But notwithstanding these flattering expressions, he appears to have felt that he had but a short time to live; and it was probably about this period that he wrote his lines on the "Prospect of Death," perhaps one of the most beautiful and affecting compositions in our language:

> " On my bed, in wakeful restlessness,
> I turn me wearisome; while all around,
> All, all, save me, sink in forgetfulness;
> I only wake to watch the sickly taper
> Which lights me to my tomb. — Yes, 't is the hand
> Of Death I feel press heavy on my vitals,
> Slow sapping the warm current of existence
> My moments now are few — the sand of life
> Ebbs fastly to its finish. Yet a little,
> And the last fleeting particle will fall,
> Silent, unseen, unnoticed, unlamented.
> Come then, sad Thought, and let us meditate
> While meditate we may.
>
> . . . . . . . . . . . .
>
> I hoped I should not leave
> The earth without a vestige; Fate decrees
> It shall be otherwise, and I submit.
> Henceforth, O world, no more of thy desires!
> No more of Hope! the wanton vagrant Hope;
> I abjure all. Now other cares engross me,
> And my tired soul, with emulative haste,
> Looks to its God, and prunes its wings for Heaven."

On the 22nd of September he wrote to Mr. Charlesworth, and his letter indicates the possession of higher spirits and more sanguine hopes, than almost any other in his correspondence. About the end of that month he went to London, on a visit to his brother Neville, but returned to College within a few weeks, in a state that precluded all chance of prolonging his existence; but still he did not cease to hope, or rather sought to delude his brother into the belief that he should recover; for in a letter addressed to him, which was found in his pocket after his decease, dated Saturday, 11th of October, he says,

"I am safely arrived, and in College, but my illness has increased upon me much. The cough continues, and is attended with a good deal of fever. I am under the care of Mr. Farish, and entertain very little apprehension about the cough; but my over-exertions in town have reduced me to a state of much debility; and, until the cough be gone, I cannot be permitted to take any strengthening medicines. This places me in an awkward predicament; but I think I perceive a degree of expectoration this morning, which will soon relieve me, and then I shall mend apace. Under these circumstances I must not expect to see you here at present; when I am a little recovered, it will be a pleasant relaxation to me. Our lectures began on Friday, but I do not attend them until I am better. I have not written to my mother, nor shall I while I remain unwell. You will tell her, as a reason, that our lectures began on Friday. I know she will be uneasy if she do not hear from me, and still more so, if I tell her I am ill.

"I cannot write more at present than that I am

"Your truly affectionate Brother,

"H. K. White."

A friend acquainted his brother with his situation, who hastened to him; but when he arrived he was delirious, and though reason returned for a few moments, as if to bless him with the consciousness that the same fond relative, to whose attachment he owed so much, was present at his last hour, he sunk into a stupor, and on Sunday, the 19th of October, 1806, he breathed his last.

Thus died, in his twenty-second year, Henry Kirke White, whose genius and virtues justified the brightest hopes, and whose fitness for Heaven does not bring the consolation for his untimely fate which perhaps it ought. It is impossible to refrain from anticipating what his talents might have produced, had his existence been extended; and though it is extremely doubtful if he were capable of worldly happiness, there is a selfishness in our nature which makes us grieve when those who are likely to increase our intellectual pleasures are hurried to the grave.

In whatever light the character of this unhappy youth be contemplated, it is full of instruction. His talents were unusually precocious, and their variety was as astonishing as their extent. Besides the Poetical pieces in this volume, and his scholastic attainments, his ability was manifested in various other ways. His style was remarkable for its clearness and elegance, and his correspondence and prose pieces show extensive information. To great genius and capacity, he united the rarest and more important gifts of sound judgment and common sense. It is usually the misfortune of genius to invest ordinary objects with a meretricious colouring, that perverts their forms and purposes, to make its possessor imagine that it exempts him from attending to those strict rules of moral conduct to which others are bound to adhere, and to render him neglectful of the sacred assurance that "to whom much is given from him will much be required." Nature, in Kirke White's case, appears, on the contrary, to have determined that she would, in one instance at least, prove that high intellectual attainments are strictly compatible with every social and moral virtue. At a very early period of his life, religion became the predominant feeling of his mind, and she imparted her sober and chastened effects to all his thoughts and actions. The cherished object of every member of his family, he repaid their affection by the most anxious solicitude for their welfare, offering his advice on spiritual affairs with impressive earnestness, and indicating, in every letter of his voluminous correspondence, the greatest consideration for their feelings and happiness. For the last six years he deemed himself marked out for the service of his Maker, not like the member of a convent, whose duties consist only in prayer, but in the exercise of that philanthropy and practical benevolence which ought to adorn every parish priest. To qualify himself properly for the holy office, he subjected his mind to the severest discipline; and his letters display a rational piety, and an enlightened view of religious obligations, that confer much greater honour upon his name, than his Poetical pieces, whether as proofs of talent, or of the qualities of his heart.

Such was Henry Kirke White as he appeared to others; but there are minuter traits of character which no observer can catch, and which the possessor must himself delineate. Though early impressed with melancholy, it was not of a misanthropic nature; and while despair and disappointment were preying on his heart, he was all sweetness and docility to others. A consciousness of the possession of abilities, and of being capable of better things than those which he seemed destined to perform, gives to some of his productions the appearance of discontent, and of having overrated his pretensions. He was, like many youthful Poets, too fond of complaining of fortune, of supposing himself neglected, and of comparing his humble lot with those situations for which he believed himself qualified; but these were the lucubrations of his earliest years, before he found friends to foster his talents. So far, indeed, from having reason to lament the indifference of others to his merits, his life affords one of the most striking examples in the history of genius, that talents when united to moral worth, will be rewarded by honours and fame, that obscure birth is no impediment to advancement, and that a person of the humblest origin may, by his own exertions, become, in the great arena of learning, an object of envy even to those of the highest rank. It is due to him, whose good sense was so remarkable, to point out the time in his career to which the passages in question refer; and to add that his correspondence, after he entered the University, expressed nothing but satisfaction with his lot, and a desire to justify the kindness and expectations of his patrons. Still, Kirke White was unhappy; and, since no other cause then existed for his mental wretchedness, it must be ascribed to a morbid temperament, induced partly by ill health, and partly by constitutional infirmity. The uncertainty of his early prospects, and the fear of ridicule if he expressed his feelings, rendered him reserved, and made him confine his thoughts to his own bosom, for he says,

> "When all was new, and life was in its spring,
> I lived an unloved solitary thing;
> E'en then I learn'd to bury deep from day
> The piercing cares that wore my youth away;

and in a letter to Mr. Maddock, in September, 1804, he thus spoke of himself:

"Perhaps it may be that I am not formed for friendship, that I expect more than can ever be found. Time will tutor me; I am a singular being under a common outside: I am a profound dissembler of my inward feelings, and necessity has taught me the art. I am long before I can unbosom to a friend, yet, I think, I am sincere in my friendship: you must not attribute this to any suspiciousness of nature, but must consider that I lived seventeen years my own confidant, my own friend, full of projects and strange thoughts, and confiding them to no one. I am habitually reserved, and habitually cautious in letting it be seen that I hide any thing."

None knew better than himself that the aspirations and feelings of which genius is the parent are often found to be inconsistent with felicity:

"Oh! hear the plaint by thy sad favourite made,
 His melancholy moan,
He tells of scorn, he tells of broken vows,
 Of sleepless nights, of anguish-ridden days,
Pangs that his sensibility uprouse
 To curse his being and his thirst for praise.
Thou gavest to him with treble force to feel
 The sting of keen neglect, the rich man's scorn;
And what o'er all does in his soul preside
 Predominant, and tempers him to steel,
  His high indignant pride."

Nor was he unconscious that the toils necessary to secure literary distinction, when endured by a shattered frame, are in the highest degree severe. How much truth and feeling are there in the Lines which he wrote after spending a whole night in study, an hour when religious impressions force themselves with irresistible weight on the exhausted mind:

"Oh! when reflecting on these truths sublime,
How insignificant do all the joys,
The gaudes, and honours of the world appear!
How vain ambition! — Why has my wakeful lamp
Outwatch'd the slow-paced night? — Why on the page,
The schoolman's labour'd page, have I employ'd

The hours devoted by the world to rest,
And needful to recruit exhausted nature?
Say, can the voice of narrow Fame repay
The loss of health? or can the hope of glory
Lend a new throb unto my languid heart,
Cool, even now, my feverish aching brow,
Relume the fires of this deep sunken eye,
Or paint new colours on this pallid cheek?"

What a picture of mental suffering does the following passage present, and how impressive does it become when the fate of the author is remembered:

"These feverish dews that on my temples hang,
This quivering lip, these eyes of dying flame;
These, the dread signs of many a secret pang—
These are the meed of him who pants for Fame!"

Like so many other ardent students, the night was his favourite time for reading; and, dangerous as the habit is to health, what student will not agree in his descriptions of the pleasures that attend it?

"The night's my own, they cannot steal my night!
When evening lights her folding star on high,
I live and breathe; and, in the sacred hours
Of quiet and repose, my spirit flies,
Free as the morning, o'er the realms of space,
And mounts the skies, and imps her wing for heaven."

Kirke White's poetry is popular, because it describes feelings, passions, and associations, which all have felt, and with which all can sympathize. It is by no means rich in metaphor, nor does it evince great powers of imagination; but it is pathetic, plaintive, and agreeable; and emanating directly from his own heart, it appeals irresistibly to that of his reader. His meaning is always clear, and the force and vigour of his expressions are remarkable. In estimating his poetical powers, however, it should be remembered, that nearly all his Poems were written before he was nineteen; and that they are, in truth, but the germs of future excellence, and ought not to be criticized as if they were the fruits of an intellect on which time and education had bestowed their advantages. It is, however, in his prose works, and especially in his correspondence, that the versatility of his talents, his acquirements, his piety, and his moral excellence are most conspicuous.

A question arises with respect to him which, in the history of a young Poet, is always interesting, but which Mr. Southey has not touched. Abundance of proof exists in his writings of the susceptibility of his heart; but it is not stated that he ever formed an attachment. In many of his pieces he speaks with tenderness of a female whom he calls Fanny; and in one of them, from which it appears that she was dead, he expresses his regard in no equivocal manner; but there are other grounds for concluding that his happiness was affected by disappointed affection. To his friend Mr. Maddock, in July, 1804, he observed:

"I shall never, never marry. It cannot, must not be. As to affections, mine are already engaged as much as they ever will be, and this is one reason why I believe my life will be a life of celibacy. I love too ardently to make love innocent, and therefore I say farewell to it."

With this passage one of his Sonnets singularly agrees:

When I sit musing on the chequer'd past
  (A term much darken'd with untimely woes),
  My thoughts revert to her, for whom still flows
The tear, though half disowned; and binding fast
Pride's stubborn cheat to my too yielding heart,
  I say to her, she robb'd me of my rest,
  When that was all my wealth. 'T is true my breast
Received from her this wearying, lingering smart;
Yet, ah! I cannot bid her form depart;
  Though wrong'd, I love her — yet in anger love,
  For she was most unworthy. Then I prove
Vindictive joy: and on my stern front gleams,
Throned in dark clouds, inflexible . . .
The native pride of my much injured heart.

Was the subject of this Sonnet wholly imaginary, or was there some unfortunate story which, for sufficient reasons, his biographers have suppressed? It is true, that in his letters, written at a much later period, he speaks of marriage in a manner not to be reconciled with the idea that he was then suffering from recollections of that description; but he may, in the interval of two years, have partially recovered from his loss.

Kirke White was buried in the Church of All Saints, Cambridge, but no monument was erected to him until a liberal minded American, Mr. Francis Boott, of Boston, placed a tablet to his memory, with a medallion, by Chantrey, with the following inscription, by Professor Smyth, one of his numerous friends:

"Warm'd with fond hope and learning's sacred flame,
To Granta's bowers the youthful Poet came;
Unconquer'd powers the immortal mind display'd,
But worn with anxious thought, the frame decay'd:
Pale o'er his lamp, and in his cell retired,
The martyr student faded and expired.
Oh! genius, taste, and piety sincere,
Too early lost 'midst studies too severe!
Foremost to mourn, was generous Southey seen,
He told the tale, and show'd what White had been,
Nor told in vain. For o'er the Atlantic wave
A wanderer came, and sought the Poet's grave;
On yon low stone he saw his lonely name,
And raised this fond memorial to his fame."

# POEMS.

# *CLIFTON GROVE.*

---

## *DEDICATION.*

*To Her Grace the Duchess of Devonshire, the following trifling effusions of a very youthful Muse are, by permission, dedicated by her Grace's much obliged and grateful Servant,*

*HENRY KIRKE WHITE*

*Nottingham.*

# PREFACE.

---

THE following attempts in Verse are laid before the Public with extreme diffidence. The Author is very conscious that the juvenile efforts of a youth, who has not received the polish of Academical discipline, and who has been but sparingly blessed with opportunities for the prosecution of scholastic pursuits, must necessarily be defective in the accuracy and finished elegance which mark the works of the man who has passed his life in the retirement of his study, furnishing his mind with images, and at the same time attaining the power of disposing those images to the best advantage.

The unpremeditated effusions of a Boy, from his thirteenth year, employed, not in the acquisition of literary information, but in the more active business of life, must not be expected to exhibit any considerable portion of the correctness of a Virgil, or the vigorous compression of a Horace.

Men are not, I believe, frequently known to bestow much labour on their amusements; and these poems were, most of them, written merely to beguile a leisure hour, or to fill up the languid intervals of studies of a severer nature.

*Πας το οικειος εργον αγαπαω*, "Every one loves his own work," says Stagyrite; but it was no overweening affection of this kind which induced this publication. Had the author relied on his own judgment only, these Poems would not, in all probability, ever have seen the light.

Perhaps it may be asked of him, what are his motives for this publication? He answers — simply these: The facilitation, through its means, of those studies which, from his earliest infancy, have been the principal objects of his ambition; and the increase of the capacity to pursue those inclinations which may one day place him in an honourable station in the scale of society.

The principal Poem in this little collection (Clifton Grove) is, he fears, deficient in numbers and harmonious coherency of parts. It is, however, merely to be regarded as a description of a nocturnal ramble in that charming retreat, accompanied with such reflections as the scene naturally suggested. It was written twelve months ago, when the Author was in his sixteenth year: — The Miscellanies are some of them the productions of a very early age. — Of the Odes, that "To an early Primrose" was written at thirteen — the others are of a later date. — The Sonnets are chiefly irregular; they have, perhaps, no other claim to that specific denomination, than that they consist only of fourteen lines.

Such are the Poems towards which I entreat the lenity of the Public. The Critic will doubtless find in them much to condemn; he may likewise possibly discover something to commend. Let him scan my faults with an indulgent eye, and in the work of that correction which I invite, let him remember he is holding the iron Mace of Criticism over the flimsy superstructure of a youth of seventeen; and, remembering that, may he forbear from crushing, by too much rigour, the painted butterfly whose transient colours may otherwise be capable of affording a moment's innocent amusement.

H. K. WHITE.

Nottingham.

# MISCELLANEOUS POEMS.

---

## CLIFTON GROVE.

### A SKETCH.

Lo ! in the west, fast fades the lingering light,
And day's last vestige takes its silent flight.
No more is heard the woodman's measured stroke,
Which with the dawn from yonder dingle broke ;
No more, hoarse clamouring o'er the uplifted head,
The crows assembling seek their wind-rock'd bed ;
Still'd is the village hum — the woodland sounds
Have ceased to echo o'er the dewy grounds,
And general silence reigns, save when below
The murmuring Trent is scarcely heard to flow ;
And save when, swung by 'nighted rustic late,
Oft, on its hinge, rebounds the jarring gate ;
Or when the sheep-bell, in the distant vale,
Breathes its wild music on the downy gale.

Now, when the rustic wears the social smile,
Released from day and its attendant toil,
And draws his household round their evening fire,
And tells the ofttold tales that never tire ;
Or, where the town's blue turrets dimly rise,
And manufacture taints the ambient skies,
The pale mechanic leaves the labouring loom,
The air-pent hold, the pestilential room,
And rushes out, impatient to begin
The stated course of customary sin :
Now, now my solitary way I bend
Where solemn groves in awful state impend :
And cliffs, that boldly rise above the plain,
Bespeak, bless'd Clifton ! thy sublime domain.
Here lonely wandering o'er the sylvan bower,
I come to pass the meditative hour ;
To bid awhile the strife of passion cease,
And woo the calms of solitude and peace.
And oh ! thou sacred Power, who rear'st on high
Thy leafy throne where wavy poplars sigh !
Genius of woodland shades ! whose mild control
Steals with resistless witchery to the soul,
Come with thy wonted ardour, and inspire
My glowing bosom with thy hallow'd fire.
And thou, too, Fancy, from thy starry sphere,
Where to the hymning orbs thou lend'st thine ear,
Do thou descend, and bless my ravish'd sight,
Veil'd in soft visions of serene delight.
At thy command the gale that passes by

Bears in its whispers mystic harmony.
Thou wavest thy wand, and lo! what forms appear!
On the dark cloud what giant shapes career!
The ghosts of Ossian skim the misty vale,
And hosts of sylphids on the moonbeams sail.
This gloomy alcove darkling to the sight,
Where meeting trees create eternal night;
Save, when from yonder stream the sunny ray,
Reflected, gives a dubious gleam of day;
Recalls, endearing to my alter'd mind,
Times, when beneath the boxen hedge reclined,
I watch'd the lapwing to her clamorous brood;
Or lured the robin to its scatter'd food;
Or woke with song the woodland echo wild,
And at each gay response delighted smiled.
How oft, when childhood threw its golden ray
Of gay romance o'er every happy day,
Here, would I run, a visionary boy,
When the hoarse tempest shook the vaulted sky,
And, fancy-led, beheld the Almighty's form
Sternly careering on the eddying storm;
And heard, while awe congeal'd my inmost soul,
His voice terrific in the thunders roll.
With secret joy I view'd with vivid glare
The vollied lightnings cleave the sullen air;
And, as the warring winds around reviled,
With awful pleasure big,—I heard and smiled.
Beloved remembrance!—Memory which endears
This silent spot to my advancing years,
Here dwells eternal peace, eternal rest,

In shades like these to live is to be bless'd.
While happiness evades the busy crowd,
In rural coverts loves the maid to shroud.
And thou too, Inspiration, whose wild flame
Shoots with electric swiftness through the frame,
Thou here dost love to sit with upturn'd eye,
And listen to the stream that murmurs by,
The woods that wave, the gray owl's silken flight,
The mellow music of the listening night.
Congenial calms more welcome to my breast
Than maddening joy in dazzling lustre dress'd,
To Heaven my prayers, my daily prayers I raise,
That ye may bless my unambitious days,
Withdrawn, remote, from all the haunts of strife,
May trace with me the lowly vale of life,
And when her banner Death shall o'er me wave,
May keep your peaceful vigils on my grave.
Now as I rove, where wide the prospect grows,
A livelier light upon my vision flows.
No more above the embracing branches meet,
No more the river gurgles at my feet,
But seen deep down the cliff's impending side,
Through hanging woods, now gleams its silver tide.
Dim is my upland path, — across the green
Fantastic shadows fling, yet oft between
The chequer'd glooms the moon her chaste ray sheds,
Where knots of bluebells droop their graceful heads,
And beds of violets, blooming 'mid the trees,
Load with waste fragrance the nocturnal breeze.

Say, why does Man, while to his opening sight
Each shrub presents a source of chaste delight,
And Nature bids for him her treasures flow,
And gives to him alone his bliss to know,
Why does he pant for Vice's deadly charms?
Why clasp the syren Pleasure to his arms?
And suck deep draughts of her voluptuous breath,
Though fraught with ruin, infamy, and death?
Could he who thus to vile enjoyment clings
Know what calm joy from purer sources springs;
Could he but feel how sweet, how free from strife,
The harmless pleasures of a harmless life,
No more his soul would pant for joys impure,
The deadly chalice would no more allure,
But the sweet potion he was wont to sip
Would turn to poison on his conscious lip.

Fair Nature! thee, in all thy varied charms,
Fain would I clasp for ever in my arms!
Thine are the sweets which never, never sate,
Thine still remain through all the storms of fate.
Though not for me, 't was Heaven's divine command
To roll in acres of paternal land,
Yet still my lot is bless'd, while I enjoy
Thine opening beauties with a lover's eye.

Happy is he, who, though the cup of bliss
Has ever shunn'd him when he thought to kiss,
Who, still in abject poverty or pain,
Can count with pleasure what small joys remain:

Though were his sight convey'd from zone to zone,
He would not find one spot of ground his own,
Yet as he looks around, he cries with glee,
These bounding prospects all were made for me:
For me yon waving fields their burden bear,
For me yon labourer guides the shining share,
While happy I in idle ease recline,
And mark the glorious visions as they shine.
This is the charm, by sages often told,
Converting all it touches into gold.
Content can soothe where'er by fortune placed,
Can rear a garden in the desert waste.

How lovely, from this hill's superior height,
Spreads the wide view before my straining sight!
O'er many a varied mile of lengthening ground,
E'en to the blue-ridged hill's remotest bound,
My ken is borne; while o'er my head serene
The silver moon illumes the misty scene:
Now shining clear, now darkening in the glade,
In all the soft varieties of shade.

Behind me, lo! the peaceful hamlet lies,
The drowsy god has seal'd the cotter's eyes.
No more, where late the social faggot blazed,
The vacant peal resounds, by little raised;
But locked in silence, o'er Arion's * star
The slumbering Night rolls on her velvet car:

* The constellation Delphinus. For authority for this appellation, see Ovid's Fasti, B. xi. 113.

The church bell tolls, deep sounding down the glade,
The solemn hour for walking spectres made;
The simple ploughboy, wakening with the sound,
Listens aghast, and turns him startled round,
Then stops his ears, and strives to close his eyes,
Lest at the sound some grisly ghost should rise.
Now ceased the long, the monitory toll,
Returning silence stagnates in the soul;
Save when, disturb'd by dreams, with wild affright,
The deep mouth'd mastiff bays the troubled night:
Or where the village alehouse crowns the vale,
The creaking signpost whistles to the gale.
A little onward let me bend my way,
Where the moss'd seat invites the traveller's stay.
That spot, oh! yet it is the very same;
That hawthorn gives it shade, and gave it name:
There yet the primrose opes its earliest bloom,
There yet the violet sheds its first perfume,
And in the branch that rears above the rest
The robin unmolested builds its nest.
'Twas here, when hope, presiding o'er my breast,
In vivid colours every prospect dress'd:
'Twas here, reclining, I indulged her dreams,
And lost the hour in visionary schemes.
Here, as I press once more the ancient seat,
Why, bland deceiver! not renew the cheat!
Say, can a few short years this change achieve,
That thy illusions can no more deceive!
Time's sombrous tints have every view o'erspread,
And thou too, gay seducer, art thou fled?

Though vain thy promise, and the suit severe,
Yet thou couldst guile Misfortune of her tear,
And oft thy smiles across life's gloomy way
Could throw a gleam of transitory day.
How gay, in youth, the flattering future seems;
How sweet is manhood in the infant's dreams;
The dire mistake too soon is brought to light,
And all is buried in redoubled night.
Yet some can rise superior to the pain,
And in their breasts the charmer Hope retain;
While others, dead to feeling, can survey,
Unmoved, their fairest prospects fade away:
But yet a few there be, — too soon o'ercast!
Who shrink unhappy from the adverse blast,
And woo the first bright gleam, which breaks the
gloom,
To gild the silent slumbers of the tomb.
So in these shades the early primrose blows,
Too soon deceived by suns and melting snows:
So falls untimely on the desert waste,
Its blossoms withering in the northern blast.

Now pass'd whate'er the upland heights display,
Down the steep cliff I wind my devious way;
Oft rousing, as the rustling path I beat,
The timid hare from its accustom'd seat.
And oh! how sweet this walk o'erhung with wood,
That winds the margin of the solemn flood!
What rural objects steal upon the sight!
What rising views prolong the calm delight!

The brooklet branching from the silver Trent,
The whispering birch by every zephyr bent,
The woody island, and the naked mead,
The lowly hut half hid in groves of reed,
The rural wicket, and the rural stile,
And frequent interspersed, the woodman's pile.
Above, below, where'er I turn my eyes,
Rocks, waters, woods, in grand succession rise.
High up the cliff the varied groves ascend,
And mournful larches o'er the wave impend.
Around, what sounds, what magic sounds arise,
What glimmering scenes salute my ravish'd eyes!
Soft sleep the waters on their pebbly bed,
The woods wave gently o'er my drooping head.
And, swelling slow, comes wafted on the wind,
Lorn Progne's note from distant copse behind.
Still every rising sound of calm delight
Stamps but the fearful silence of the night,
Save when is heard between each dreary rest,
Discordant from her solitary nest,
The owl, dull screaming to the wandering moon;
Now riding, cloud-wrapp'd, near her highest noon:
Or when the wild duck, southering, hither rides,
And plunges sullen in the sounding tides.

How oft, in this sequester'd spot, when youth
Gave to each tale the holy force of truth,
Have I long linger'd, while the milkmaid sung
The tragic legend, till the woodland rung!
That tale, so sad! which, still to memory dear,

From its sweet source can call the sacred tear,
And (lull'd to rest stern Reason's harsh control)
Steal its soft magic to the passive soul. [wind,
These hallow'd shades, — these trees that woo the
Recall its faintest features to my mind.
A hundred passing years, with march sublime,
Have swept beneath the silent wing of time,
Since, in yon hamlet's solitary shade,
Reclusely dwelt the far famed Clifton Maid,
The beauteous Margaret; for her each swain
Confess'd in private his peculiar pain,
In secret sigh'd, a victim to despair,
Nor dared to hope to win the peerless fair.
No more the Shepherd on the blooming mead
Attuned to gaiety his artless reed,
No more entwined the pansied wreath, to deck
His favourite wether's unpolluted neck,
But listless, by yon bubbling stream reclined,
He mix'd his sobbings with the passing wind,
Bemoan'd his hapless love; or, boldly bent,
Far from these smiling fields a rover went,
O'er distant lands, in search of ease, to roam,
A self-will'd exile from his native home.

Yet not to all the maid express'd disdain;
Her Bateman loved, nor loved the youth in vain.
Full oft, low whispering o'er these arching boughs,
The echoing vault responded to their vows,
As here deep hidden from the glare of day,
Enamour'd oft, they took their secret way.

Yon bosky dingle, still the rustics name;
'T was there the blushing maid confess'd her flame.
Down yon green lane they oft were seen to hie,
When evening slumber'd on the western sky.
That blasted yew, that mouldering walnut bare,
Each bears mementos of the fated pair.

One eve, when Autumn loaded every breeze
With the fallen honours of the mourning trees,
The maiden waited at the accustom'd bower,
And waited long beyond the appointed hour,
Yet Bateman came not; — o'er the woodland drear,
Howling portentous did the winds career;
And bleak and dismal on the leafless woods
The fitful rains rush'd down in sullen floods;
The night was dark; as, now and then, the gale
Paused for a moment — Margaret listen'd pale;
But through the covert to her anxious ear
No rustling footstep spoke her lover near. [why,
Strange fears now fill'd her breast, — she knew not
She sigh'd, and Bateman's name was in each sigh.
She hears a noise, — 't is he, — he comes at last, —
Alas! 't was but the gale which hurried past:
But now she hears a quickening footstep sound,
Lightly it comes, and nearer does it bound;
'T is Bateman's self, — he springs into her arms,
'T is he that clasps, and chides her vain alarms.
"Yet why this silence? — I have waited long,
And the cold storm has yell'd the trees among.

And now thou'rt here my fears are fled — yet speak,
Why does the salt tear moisten on thy cheek?
Say, what is wrong?" Now through a parting cloud
The pale moon peer'd from her tempestuous shroud,
And Bateman's face was seen; 't was deadly white,
And sorrow seem'd to sicken in his sight.
"Oh, speak! my love!" again the maid conjured,
"Why is thy heart in sullen woe immured?"
He raised his head, and thrice essay'd to tell,
Thrice from his lips the unfinish'd accents fell;
When thus at last reluctantly he broke
His boding silence, and the maid bespoke:
"Grieve not, my love, but ere the morn advance
I on these fields must cast my parting glance;
For three long years, by cruel fate's command,
I go to languish in a foreign land.
Oh, Margaret! omens dire have met my view,
Say, when far distant, wilt thou bear me true?
Should honours tempt thee, and should riches fee,
Wouldst thou forget thine ardent vows to me,
And on the silken couch of wealth reclined,
Banish thy faithful Bateman from thy mind?"

"Oh! why," replies the maid, "my faith thus prove,
Canst thou! ah, canst thou, then suspect my love?
Hear me, just God! if from my traitorous heart
My Bateman's fond remembrance e'er shall part,
If, when he hail again his native shore,
He finds his Margaret true to him no more,

May fiends of hell, and every power of dread,
Conjoin'd then drag me from my perjured bed,
And hurl me headlong down these awful steeps,
To find deserved death in yonder deeps!" *
Thus spake the maid, and from her finger drew
A golden ring, and broke it quick in two;
One half she in her lovely bosom hides,
The other, trembling, to her love confides.
"This bind the vow," she said, "this mystic charm
No future recantation can disarm,
The right vindictive does the fates involve,
No tears can move it, no regrets dissolve."

She ceased. The death-bird gave a dismal cry,
The river moan'd, the wild gale whistled by,
And once again the lady of the night
Behind a heavy cloud withdrew her light.
Trembling she view'd these portents with dismay;
But gently Bateman kiss'd her fears away:
Yet still he felt conceal'd a secret smart,
Still melancholy bodings fill'd his heart.

When to the distant land the youth was sped,
A lonely life the moody maiden led. [walk,
Still would she trace each dear, each well known
Still by the moonlight to her love would talk,
And fancy, as she paced among the trees,
She heard his whispers in the dying breeze.

* This part of the Trent is commonly called "The Clifton Deeps."

Thus two years glided on in silent grief;
The third her bosom own'd the kind relief:
Absence had cool'd her love — the impoverish'd flame
Was dwindling fast, when lo! the tempter came;
He offered wealth, and all the joys of life,
And the weak maid became another's wife!
Six guilty months had mark'd the false one's crime,
When Bateman hail'd once more his native clime.
Sure of her constancy, elate he came,
The lovely partner of his soul to claim;
Light was his heart, as up the well known way
He bent his steps — and all his thoughts were gay.
Oh! who can paint his agonizing throes,
When on his ear the fatal news arose!
Chill'd with amazement, — senseless with the blow,
He stood a marble monument of woe;
Till call'd to all the horrors of despair,
He smote his brow, and tore his horrent hair;
Then rush'd impetuous from the dreadful spot,
And sought those scenes (by memory ne'er forgot),
Those scenes, the witness of their growing flame,
And now like witnesses of Margaret's shame.
'T was night—he sought the river's lonely shore,
And traced again their former wanderings o'er.
Now on the bank in silent grief he stood,
And gazed intently on the stealing flood,
Death in his mein and madness in his eye,
He watch'd the waters as they murmur'd by;
Bade the base murderess triumph o'er his grave —
Prepared to plunge into the whelming wave.

Yet still he stood irresolutely bent,
Religion sternly stay'd his rash intent.
He knelt. — Cool play'd upon his cheek the wind,
And fann'd the fever of his maddening mind,
The willows waved, the stream it sweetly swept,
The paly moonbeam on its surface slept,
And all was peace; — he felt the general calm
O'er his rack'd bosom shed a genial balm:
When casting far behind his streaming eye,
He saw the Grove, — in fancy saw her lie,
His Margaret, lull'd in Germain's * arms to rest,
And all the demon rose within his breast.
Convulsive now, he clench'd his trembling hand,
Cast his dark eye once more upon the land,
Then, at one spring he spurn'd the yielding bank,
And in the calm deceitful current sank.

Sad, on the solitude of night, the sound,
As in the stream he plunged, was heard around:
Then all was still — the wave was rough no more,
The river swept as sweetly as before;
The willows waved, the moonbeams shone serene,
And peace returning brooded o'er the scene.

Now, see upon the perjured fair one hang
Remorse's glooms and never ceasing pang.
Full well she knew, repentant now too late,
She soon must bow beneath the stroke of fate.
But, for the babe she bore beneath her breast,

* Germain is the traditionary name of her husband.

The offended God prolong'd her life unbless'd.
But fast the fleeting moments roll'd away,
And near and nearer drew the dreaded day;
That day foredoom'd to give her child the light,
And hurl its mother to the shades of night.
The hour arrived, and from the wretched wife
The guiltless baby struggled into life.—
As night drew on, around her bed a band
Of friends and kindred kindly took their stand;
In holy prayer they pass'd the creeping time,
Intent to expiate her awful crime.
Their prayers were fruitless.—As the midnight came
A heavy sleep oppress'd each weary frame.
In vain they strove against the o'erwhelming load,
Some power unseen their drowsy lids bestrode.
They slept till in the blushing eastern sky
The blooming Morning oped her dewy eye;
Then wakening wide they sought the ravish'd bed,
But lo! the hapless Margaret was fled;
And never more the weeping train were doom'd
To view the false one, in the deeps intomb'd.

The neighbouring rustics told that in the night
They heard such screams as froze them with affright;
And many an infant, at its mother's breast,
Started dismay'd, from its unthinking rest.
And even now, upon the heath forlorn,
They show the path down which the fair was borne,
By the fell demons, to the yawning wave,
Her own, and murder'd lover's, mutual grave.

Such is the tale, so sad, to memory dear,
Which oft in youth has charm'd my listening ear,
That tale, which bade me find redoubled sweets
In the drear silence of these dark retreats;
And even now, with melancholy power,
Adds a new pleasure to the lonely hour.
'Mid all the charms by magic Nature given
To this wild spot, this sublunary heaven,
With double joy enthusiast Fancy leans
On the attendant legend of the scenes.
This sheds a fairy lustre on the floods,
And breathes a mellower gloom upon the woods;
This, as the distant cataract swells around,
Gives a romantic cadence to the sound;
This, and the deepening glen, the alley green,
The silver stream, with sedgy tufts between,
The massy rock, the wood-encompass'd leas,
The broom-clad islands, and the nodding trees,
The lengthening vista, and the present gloom,
The verdant pathway breathing waste perfume:
These are thy charms, the joys which these impart
Bind thee, bless'd Clifton! close around my heart.

Dear Native Grove! where'er my devious track,
To thee will Memory lead the wanderer back.
Whether in Arno's polish'd vales I stray,
Or where "Oswego's" swamps obstruct the day;
Or wander lone, where, wildering and wide,
The tumbling torrent laves St. Gothard's side;

Or by old Tejo's classic margent muse,
Or stand entranced with Pyrenean views;
Still, still to thee, where'er my footsteps roam,
My heart shall point, and lead the wanderer home.
When Splendour offers, and when Fame incites,
I 'll pause, and think of all thy dear delights,
Reject the boon, and, wearied with the change,
Renounce the wish which first induced to range;
Turn to these scenes, these well known scenes once more,
Trace once again old Trent's romantic shore,
And tired with worlds, and all their busy ways,
Here waste the little remnant of my days.
But if the Fates should this last wish deny,
And doom me on some foreign shore to die;
Oh! should it please the world's supernal King,
That weltering waves my funeral dirge shall sing;
Or that my corse should, on some desert strand,
Lie stretch'd beneath the Simoom's blasting hand;
Still, though unwept I find a stranger tomb,
My sprite shall wander through this favourite gloom,
Ride on the wind that sweeps the leafless grove,
Sigh on the wood-blast of the dark alcove,
Sit a lorn spectre on yon well known grave,
And mix its moanings with the desert wave.

## TIME,

### A POEM.*

Genius of musings, who, the midnight hour
Wasting in woods or haunted forests wild,
Dost watch Orion in his arctic tower,
Thy dark eye fix'd as in some holy trance;
Or when the vollied lightnings cleave the air,
And Ruin gaunt bestrides the winged storm,
Sitt'st in some lonely watchtower, where thy lamp,
Faint blazing, strikes the fisher's eye from far,
And, 'mid the howl of elements, unmoved,
Dost ponder on the awful scene, and trace
The vast effect to its superior source,—
Spirit, attend my lowly benison!
For now I strike to themes of import high
The solitary lyre; and, borne by thee
Above this narrow cell, I celebrate
The mysteries of Time!
                                        Him who, august,
Was e'er these worlds were fashion'd,—ere the sun
Sprang from the east, or Lucifer display'd
His glowing cresset in the arch of morn,
Or Vesper gilded the serener eve.

* This Poem was begun either during the publication of Clifton Grove, or shortly afterwards, but never completed: some of the detached parts were among his latest productions.

Yea, He had been for an eternity!
Had swept unvarying from eternity
The harp of desolation — ere his tones,
At God's command, assumed a milder strain,
And startled on his watch, in the vast deep,
Chaos's sluggish sentry, and evoked
From the dark void the smiling universe.

Chain'd to the groveling frailties of the flesh,
Mere mortal man, unpurged from earthly dross,
Cannot survey, with fix'd and steady eye,
The dim uncertain gulf, which now the muse,
Adventurous, would explore; but dizzy grown,
He topples down the abyss. — If he would scan
The fearful chasm, and catch a transient glimpse
Of its unfathomable depths, that so
His mind may turn with double joy to God,
His only certainty and resting place;
He must put off awhile this mortal vest,
And learn to follow, without giddiness,
To heights where all is vision, and surprise,
And vague conjecture. — He must waste by night
The studious taper, far from all resort
Of crowds and folly, in some still retreat;
High on the beetling promontory's crest,
Or in the caves of the vast wilderness,
Where, compass'd round with Nature's wildest shapes,
He may be driven to centre all his thoughts
In the great Architect, who lives confess'd
In rocks, and seas, and solitary wastes.

So has divine Philosophy, with voice
Mild as the murmurs of the moonlight wave,
Tutor'd the heart of him, who now awakes,
Touching the chords of solemn minstrelsy,
His faint, neglected song — intent to snatch
Some vagrant blossom from the dangerous steep
Of poesy, a bloom of such a hue,
So sober, as may not unseemly suit
With Truth's severer brow; and one withal
So hardy as shall brave the passing wind
Of many winters, — rearing its meek head
In loveliness, when he who gather'd it
Is number'd with the generations gone.
Yet not to me hath God's good providence
Given studious leisure,* or unbroken thought,
Such as he owns, — a meditative man;
Who from the blush of morn to quiet eve
Ponders, or turns the page of wisdom o'er,
Far from the busy crowd's tumultuous din:
From noise and wrangling far, and undisturb'd
With Mirth's unholy shouts. For me the day
Hath duties which require the vigorous hand
Of steadfast application, but which leave
No deep improving trace upon the mind.
But be the day another's; — let it pass!
The night's my own! — They cannot steal my night!
When evening lights her folding star on high,
I live and breathe; and in the sacred hours

* The Author was then in an attorney's office.

Of quiet and repose my spirit flies,
Free as the morning, o'er the realms of space,
And mounts the skies, and imps her wing for Heaven.

Hence do I love the sober-suited maid;
Hence Night's my friend, my mistress, and my theme,
And she shall aid me now to magnify
The night of ages, — now when the pale ray
Of starlight penetrates the studious gloom,
And, at my window seated, while mankind
Are lock'd in sleep, I feel the freshening breeze
Of stillness blow, while, in her saddest stole,
Thought, like a wakeful vestal at her shrine,
Assumes her wonted sway.
Behold the world
Rests, and her tired inhabitants have paused
From trouble and turmoil. The widow now
Has ceased to weep, and her twin orphans lie
Lock'd in each arm, partakers of her rest.
The man of sorrow has forgot his woes;
The outcast that his head is shelterless,
His griefs unshared. — The mother tends no more
Her daughter's dying slumbers, but surprised
With heaviness, and sunk upon her couch,
Dreams of her bridals. Even the hectic, lull'd
On Death's lean arm to rest, in visions wrapp'd,
Crowning with Hope's bland wreath his shuddering nurse,
Poor victim! smiles. — Silence and deep repose
Reign o'er the nations; and the warning voice

Of Nature utters audibly within
The general moral: — tells us that repose,
Deathlike as this, but of far longer span,
Is coming on us — that the weary crowds,
Who now enjoy a temporary calm,
Shall soon taste lasting quiet, wrapp'd around
With grave clothes: and their aching restless heads
Mouldering in holes and corners unobserved,
Till the last trump shall break their sullen sleep.

Who needs a teacher to admonish him
That flesh is grass, that earthly things are mist?
What are our joys but dreams? and what our hopes
But goodly shadows in the summer cloud?
There's not a wind that blows but bears with it
Some rainbow promise: — Not a moment flies
But puts its sickle in the fields of life,
And mows its thousands, with their joys and cares.
'T is but as yesterday since on yon stars,
Which now I view, the Chaldee shepherd * gazed
In his mid watch observant, and disposed
The twinkling hosts as fancy gave them shape.
Yet in the interim what mighty shocks
Have buffeted mankind — whole nations razed —
Cities made desolate — the polish'd sunk
To barbarism, and once barbaric states
Swaying the wand of science and of arts;
Illustrious deeds and memorable names

* Alluding to the first astronomical observations made by the Chaldean shepherds.

Blotted from record, and upon the tongue
Of gray Tradition, voluble no more.

Where are the heroes of the ages past?
Where the brave chieftains, where the mighty ones
Who flourish'd in the infancy of days?
All to the grave gone down. On their fallen fame
Exultant, mocking at the pride of man,
Sits grim Forgetfulness. — The warrior's arm
Lies nerveless on the pillow of its shame;
Hush'd is his stormy voice, and quench'd the blaze
Of his red eyeball. — Yesterday his name
Was mighty on the earth. — To-day — 't is what?
The meteor of the night of distant years,
That flash'd unnoticed, save by wrinkled eld,
Musing at midnight upon prophecies,
Who at her lonely lattice saw the gleam
Point to the mist-poised shroud, then quietly
Closed her pale lips, and lock'd the secret up
Safe in the charnel's treasures.
Oh how weak
Is mortal man! how trifling — how confined
His scope of vision! Puff'd with confidence,
His phrase grows big with immortality,
And he, poor insect of a summer's day!
Dreams of eternal honours to his name;
Of endless glory and perennial bays.
He idly reasons of eternity,
As of the train of ages, — when, alas!
Ten thousand thousand of his centuries

Are, in comparison, a little point
Too trivial for account. — O, it is strange,
'T is passing strange, to mark his fallacies;
Behold him proudly view some pompous pile,
Whose high dome swells to emulate the skies,
And smile, and say, My name shall live with this
Till time shall be no more; while at his feet,
Yea, at his very feet, the crumbling dust
Of the fallen fabric of the other day
Preaches the solemn lesson. — He should know
That time must conquer; that the loudest blast
That ever fill'd Renown's obstreperous trump
Fades in the lapse of ages, and expires.
Who lies inhumed in the terrific gloom
Of the gigantic pyramid? or who
Rear'd its huge walls? Oblivion laughs, and says,
The prey is mine. — They sleep, and never more
Their names shall strike upon the ear of man,
Their memory burst its fetters.
Where is Rome?
She lives but in the tale of other times;
Her proud pavilions are the hermit's home,
And her long colonnades, her public walks,
Now faintly echo to the pilgrim's feet,
Who comes to muse in solitude, and trace,
Through the rank moss reveal'd, her honour'd dust.
But not to Rome alone has fate confined
The doom of ruin; cities numberless,
Tyre, Sidon, Carthage, Babylon, and Troy,

And rich Phœnicia — they are blotted out,
Half razed from memory, and their very name
And being in dispute. — Has Athens fallen?
Is polish'd Greece become the savage seat
Of ignorance and sloth? and shall we dare

. . . . . . . . . . . . . .
. . . . . . . . . . . . . .
. . . . . . . . . . . . . .

And empire seeks another hemisphere.
Where now is Britain? — Where her laurel'd names.
Her palaces and halls? Dash'd in the dust.
Some second Vandal hath reduced her pride,
And with one big recoil hath thrown her back
To primitive barbarity. —— Again,
Through her depopulated vales, the scream
Of bloody Superstition hollow rings,
And the scared native to the tempest howls
The yell of deprecation. O'er her marts,
Her crowded ports, broods Silence; and the cry
Of the low curlew, and the pensive dash
Of distant billows, breaks alone the void;
Even as the savage sits upon the stone
That marks where stood her capitols, and hears
The bittern booming in the weeds, he shrinks
From the dismaying solitude. — Her bards
Sing in a language that hath perished;
And their wild harps suspended o'er their graves,
Sigh to the desert winds a dying strain.

Meanwhile the Arts, in second infancy,
Rise in some distant clime, and then, perchance,
Some bold adventurer, fill'd with golden dreams,
Steering his bark through trackless solitudes,
Where, to his wandering thoughts, no daring prow
Hath ever plough'd before,—espies the cliffs
Of fallen Albion.—To the land unknown
He journeys joyful; and perhaps descries
Some vestige of her ancient stateliness:
Then he, with vain conjecture, fills his mind
Of the unheard-of race, which had arrived
At science in that solitary nook,
Far from the civil world; and sagely sighs,
And moralizes on the state of man.

Still on its march, unnoticed and unfelt,
Moves on our being. We do live and breathe,
And we are gone. The spoiler heeds us not.
We have our springtime and our rottenness;
And as we fall, another race succeeds,
To perish likewise.—Meanwhile Nature smiles—
The seasons run their round—The Sun fulfils
His annual course—and heaven and earth remain
Still changing, yet unchanged—still doom'd to feel
Endless mutation in perpetual rest.
Where are conceal'd the days which have elapsed?
Hid in the mighty cavern of the past,
They rise upon us only to appall,
By indistinct and half-glimpsed images,
Misty, gigantic, huge, obsure, remote.

Oh, it is fearful, on the midnight couch,
When the rude rushing winds forget to rave,
And the pale moon, that through the casement high
Surveys the sleepless muser, stamps the hour
Of utter silence, it is fearful then
To steer the mind, in deadly solitude,
Up the vague stream of probability;
To wind the mighty secrets of the past,
And turn the key of time! — Oh! who can strive
To comprehend the vast, the awful truth,
Of the eternity that hath gone by,
And not recoil from the dismaying sense
Of human impotence? The life of man
Is summ'd in birthdays and in sepulchres;
But the Eternal God had no beginning;
He hath no end. Time had been with him
For everlasting, ere the dædal world
Rose from the gulf in loveliness. — Like him
It knew no source, like him, 't was uncreate.
What is it then? The past Eternity!
We comprehend a future without end;
We feel it possible that even yon sun
May roll for ever: but we shrink amazed —
We stand aghast, when we reflect that time
Knew no commencement. — That heap age on age,
And million upon million, without end,
And we shall never span the void of days
That were and are not but in retrospect.
The Past is an unfathomable depth,
Beyond the span of thought; 'tis an elapse

Which hath no mensuration, but hath been
For ever and for ever.
Change of days
To us is sensible; and each revolve
Of the recording sun conducts us on
Further in life, and nearer to our goal.
Not so with Time, — mysterious chronicler,
He knoweth not mutation; — centuries
Are to his being as a day, and days
As centuries. — Time past, and Time to come,
Are always equal; when the world began
God had existed from eternity.

. . . . . . . . .

Now look on man
Myriads of ages hence. — Hath time elapsed?
Is he not standing in the selfsame place
Where once we stood? — The same eternity
Hath gone before him, and is yet to come;
His past is not of longer span than ours,
Though myriads of ages intervened;
For who can add to what has neither sum,
Nor bound, nor source, nor estimate, nor end?
Oh, who can compass the Almighty mind?
Who can unlock the secrets of the high?
In speculations of an altitude
Sublime as this, our reason stands confess'd
Foolish, and insignificant, and mean.
Who can apply the futile argument
Of finite beings to infinity?

He might as well compress the universe
Into the hollow compass of a gourd,
Scoop'd out by human art; or bid the whale
Drink up the sea it swims in! — Can the less
Contain the greater? or the dark obscure
Infold the glories of meridian day?
What does philosophy impart to man
But undiscover'd wonders? — Let her soar
Even to her proudest heights — to where she caught
The soul of Newton and of Socrates,
She but extends the scope of wild amaze
And admiration. All her lessons end
In wider views of God's unfathom'd depths.

Lo! the unletter'd hind, who never knew
To raise his mind excursive to the heights
Of abstract contemplation, as he sits
On the green hillock by the hedge-row side,
What time the insect swarms are murmuring,
And marks, in silent thought, the broken clouds
That fringe with loveliest hues the evening sky,
Feels in his soul the hand of Nature rouse
The thrill of gratitude, to him who form'd
The goodly prospect; he beholds the God
Throned in the west, and his reposing ear
Hears sounds angelic in the fitful breeze
That floats through neighbouring copse or fairy brake,
Or lingers playful on the haunted stream.
Go with the cotter to his winter fire,
Where o'er the moors the loud blast whistles shrill,

And the hoarse ban-dog bays the icy moon;
Mark with what awe he lists the wild uproar,
Silent, and big with thought; and hear him bless
The God that rides on the tempestuous clouds,
For his snug hearth, and all his little joys:
Hear him compare his happier lot with his
Who bends his way across the wintry wolds,
A poor night traveller, while the dismal snow
Beats in his face, and, dubious of his path,
He stops, and thinks, in every lengthening blast,
He hears some village mastiff's distant howl,
And sees, far streaming, some lone cottage light;
Then, undeceived, upturns his streaming eyes,
And clasps his shivering hands; or overpower'd,
Sinks on the frozen ground, weigh'd down with sleep,
From which the hapless wretch shall never wake.
Thus the poor rustic warms his heart with praise
And glowing gratitude,—he turns to bless,
With honest warmth, his Maker and his God!
And shall it e'er be said, that a poor hind,
Nursed in the lap of Ignorance, and bred
In want and labour, glows with nobler zeal
To laud his Maker's attributes, while he
Whom starry Science in her cradle rock'd,
And Castaly enchasten'd with his dews,
Closes his eyes upon the holy word,
And, blind to all but arrogance and pride,
Dares to declare his infidelity,
And openly contemn the Lord of Hosts?
What is philosophy, if it impart

Irreverence for the Deity, or teach
A mortal man to set his judgment up
Against his Maker's will? The Polygar,
Who kneels to sun or moon, compared with him
Who thus perverts the talents he enjoys,
Is the most bless'd of men! Oh! I would walk
A weary journey, to the furthest verge
Of the big world, to kiss that good man's hand,
Who, in the blaze of wisdom and of art,
Preserves a lowly mind; and to his God,
Feeling the sense of his own littleness,
Is as a child in meek simplicity!
What is the pomp of learning? the parade
Of letters and of tongues? e'en as the mists
Of the gray morn before the rising sun,
That pass away and perish.
Earthly things
Are but the transient pageants of an hour;
And earthly pride is like the passing flower,
That springs to fall, and blossoms but to die.
'T is as the tower erected on a cloud,
Baseless and silly as the schoolboy's dream.
Ages and epochs that destroy our pride,
And then record its downfall, what are they
But the poor creatures of man's teeming brain?
Hath Heaven its ages? or doth Heaven preserve
Its stated eras? Doth the Omnipotent
Hear of to-morrows or of yesterdays?
There is to God nor future nor a past;
Throned in his might, all times to him are present;

He hath no lapse, no past, no time to come;
He sees before him one eternal now.
Time moveth not! — our being 't is that moves;
And we, swift gliding down life's rapid stream,
Dream of swift ages and revolving years,
Ordain'd to chronicle our passing days:
So the young sailor in the gallant bark,
Scudding before the wind, beholds the coast
Receding from his eyes, and thinks the while,
Struck with amaze, that he is motionless,
And that the land is sailing.
                                        Such, alas!
Are the illusions of this proteus life!
All, all is false: through every phasis still
'T is shadowy and deceitful. It assumes
The semblances of things and specious shapes;
But the lost traveller might as soon rely
On the evasive spirit of the marsh,
Whose lantern beams, and vanishes, and flits,
O'er bog, and rock, and pit, and hollow way,
As we on its appearances.
                                        On earth
There is no certainty nor stable hope.
As well the weary mariner, whose bark
Is toss'd beyond Cimmerian Bosphorus,
Where storm and darkness hold their drear domain,
And sunbeams never penetrate, might trust
To expectation of serener skies,
And linger in the very jaws of death,
Because some peevish cloud were opening,

Or the loud storm had bated in its rage;
As we look forward in this vale of tears
To permanent delight — from some slight glimpse
Of shadowy, unsubstantial happiness.

The good man's hope is laid far, far beyond
The sway of tempests, or the furious sweep
Of mortal desolation. — He beholds
Unapprehensive, the gigantic stride
Of rampant Ruin, or the unstable waves
Of dark Vicissitude. — Even in death, —
In that dread hour, when, with a giant pang,
Tearing the tender fibres of the heart,
The immortal spirit struggles to be free,
Then, even then, that hope forsakes him not,
For it exists beyond the narrow verge
Of the cold sepulchre. The petty joys
Of fleeting life indignantly it spurn'd,
And rested on the bosom of its God.
This is man's only reasonable hope;
And 't is a hope which, cherish'd in the breast,
Shall not be disappointed. Even he,
The Holy One — Almighty — who clanced
The rolling world along its airy way,
Even He will deign to smile upon the good,
And welcome him to these celestial seats,
Where joy and gladness hold their changeless reign

Thou, proud man, look upon yon starry vault,
Survey the countless gems which richly stud

The night's imperial chariot; — Telescopes
Will show thee myriads more innumerous
Than the sea sand; — each of those little lamps
Is the great source of light, the central sun
Round which some other mighty sisterhood
Of planets travel, every planet stock'd
With living beings impotent as thee.
Now, proud man! now, where is thy greatness fled?
What art thou in the scale of universe?
Less, less than nothing! — Yet of thee the God
Who built this wondrous frame of worlds is careful,
As well as of the mendicant who begs
The leavings of thy table. And shalt thou
Lift up thy thankless spirit, and contemn
His heavenly providence! Deluded fool,
Even now the thunderbolt is wing'd with death,
Even now thou totterest on the brink of hell.

How insignificant is mortal man,
Bound to the hasty pinions of an hour!
How poor, how trivial in the vast conceit
Of infinite duration, boundless space!
God of the universe! Almighty One!
Thou who dost walk upon the winged winds,
Or with the storm, thy rugged charioteer,
Swift and impetuous as the northern blast,
Ridest from pole to pole; Thou who dost hold
The forked lightnings in thine awful grasp,
And reignest in the earthquake, when thy wrath
Goes down towards erring man, I would address

To thee my parting pæan; for of Thee,
Great beyond comprehension, who thyself
Art Time and Space, sublime Infinitude,
Of Thee has been my song! — With awe I kneel
Trembling before the footstool of thy state,
My God! — my Father! — I will sing to thee
A hymn of laud, a solemn canticle,
Ere on the cypress wreath, which overshades
The throne of Death, I hang my mournful lyre,
And give its wild strings to the desert gale.
Rise, Son of Salem! rise, and join the strain,
Sweep to accordant tones thy tuneful harp,
And, leaving vain laments, arouse thy soul
To exultation. Sing hosanna, sing,
And halleluiah, for the Lord is great,
And full of mercy! He has thought of man;
Yea, compass'd round with countless worlds, has thought
Of us poor worms, that batten in the dews
Of morn, and perish ere the noonday sun.
Sing to the Lord, for he is merciful:
He gave the Nubian lion but to live,
To rage its hour, and perish; but on man
He lavish'd immortality and Heaven.
The eagle falls from her aërial tower,
And mingles with irrevocable dust:
But man from death springs joyful,
Springs up to life and to eternity.
Oh, that, insensate of the favouring boon,
The great exclusive privilege bestow'd

On us unworthy trifles, men should dare
To treat with slight regard the proffer'd Heaven,
And urge the lenient, but All-Just, to swear
In wrath, " They shall not enter in my rest."
Might I address the supplicative strain
To thy high footstool, I would pray that thou
Wouldst pity the deluded wanderers,
And fold them, ere they perish, in thy flock.
Yea, I would bid thee pity them, through Him,
Thy well beloved, who, upon the cross,
Bled a dread sacrifice for human sin,
And paid, with bitter agony, the debt
Of primitive transgression.
Oh! I shrink,
My very soul doth shrink, when I reflect
That the time hastens, when, in vengeance clothed,
Thou shalt come down to stamp the seal of fate
On erring mortal man. Thy chariot wheels
Then shall rebound to earth's remotest caves,
And stormy Ocean from his bed shall start
At the appalling summons. Oh! how dread,
On the dark eye of miserable man,
Chasing his sins in secrecy and gloom,
Will burst the effulgence of the opening Heaven;
When to the brazen trumpet's deafening roar
Thou and thy dazzling cohorts shall descend,
Proclaiming the fulfilment of the word!
The dead shall start astonish'd from their sleep!
The sepulchres shall groan and yield their prey,
The bellowing floods shall disembogue their charge

Of human victims. From the farthest nook
Of the wide world shall troop the risen souls,
From him whose bones are bleaching in the waste
Of polar solitudes, or him whose corpse,
Whelm'd in the loud Atlantic's vexed tides,
Is wash'd on some Caribbean prominence,
To the lone tenant of some secret cell
In the Pacific's vast . . . . realm,
Where never plummet's sound was heard to part
The wilderness of water; they shall come
To greet the solemn advent of the Judge.

Thou first shalt summon the elected saints
To their apportion'd Heaven! and thy Son,
At thy right hand, shall smile with conscious joy
On all his past distresses, when for them
He bore humanity's severest pangs.
Then shalt thou seize the avenging scimitar,
And, with a roar as loud and horrible
As the stern earthquake's monitory voice,
The wicked shall be driven to their abode,
Down the immitigable gulf, to wail
And gnash their teeth in endless agony.

. . . . . . . .

Rear thou aloft thy standard. — Spirit, rear
Thy flag on high! — Invincible, and throned
In unparticipated might. Behold
Earth's proudest boasts, beneath thy silent sway,
Sweep headlong to destruction, thou the while,

Unmoved and heedless, thou dost hear the rush
Of mighty generations, as they pass
To the broad gulf of ruin, and dost stamp
Thy signet on them, and they rise no more.
Who shall contend with Time — unvanquish'd Time,
The conqueror of conquerors, and lord
Of desolation? — Lo! the shadows fly,
The hours and days, and years and centuries,
They fly, they fly, and nations rise and fall,
The young are old, the old are in their graves.
Heard'st thou that shout? It rent the vaulted skies;
It was the voice of people, — mighty crowds, —
Again! 'tis hushed — Time speaks, and all is hush'd;
In the vast multitude now reigns alone
Unruffled solitude. They all are still;
All — yea, the whole — the incalculable mass,
Still as the ground that clasps their cold remains.

Rear thou aloft thy standard. — Spirit, rear
Thy flag on high, and glory in thy strength.
But do thou know the season yet shall come,
When from its base thine adamantine throne
Shall tumble; when thine arm shall cease to strike,
Thy voice forget its petrifying power;
When saints shall shout, and Time shall be no more.
Yea, he doth come — the mighty champion comes,
Whose potent spear shall give thee thy death wound,
Shall crush the conqueror of conquerors,
And desolate stern Desolation's lord.
Lo! where he cometh! the Messiah comes!

The King! the Comforter! the Christ! — He comes
To burst the bonds of Death, and overturn
The power of Time. — Hark! the trumpet's blast
Rings o'er the heavens! They rise, the myriads rise —
Even from their graves they spring, and burst the chains
Of torpor, — He has ransom'd them, . . .

Forgotten generations live again,
Assume the bodily shapes they own'd of old,
Beyond the flood: — the righteous of their times
Embrace and weep, they weep the tears of joy.
The sainted mother wakes, and in her lap
Clasps her dear babe, the partner of her grave,
And heritor with her of Heaven, — a flower
Wash'd by the blood of Jesus from the stain
Of native guilt, even in its early bud.
And, hark! those strains, how solemnly serene
They fall, as from the skies — at distance fall —
Again more loud — the halleluiahs swell;
The newly risen catch the joyful sound;
They glow, they burn; and now with one accord
Bursts forth sublime from every mouth the song
Of praise to God on high, and to the Lamb
Who bled for mortals.

. . . . . . . . . . .

Yet there is peace for man. — Yea, there is peace
Even in this noisy, this unsettled scene;

When from the crowd, and from the city far,
Haply he may be set (in his late walk
O'ertaken with deep thought) beneath the boughs
Of honeysuckle, when the sun is gone,
And with fix'd eye, and wistful, he surveys
The solemn shadows of the Heavens sail,
And thinks the season yet shall come, when Time
Will waft him to repose, to deep repose,
Far from the unquietness of life — from noise
And tumult far — beyond the flying clouds,
Beyond the stars, and all this passing scene,
Where change shall cease, and Time shall be no more.

. . . . . . . . . .

## CHILDHOOD.*

### A POEM.

### PART I.

Pictured in memory's mellowing glass, how sweet
Our infant days, our infant joys, to greet;
To roam in fancy in each cherish'd scene,
The village churchyard, and the village green,
The woodland walk remote, the greenwood glade,
The mossy seat beneath the hawthorn shade,

* This appears to be one of the Author's earliest productions: written when about the age of fourteen.

The whitewash'd cottage, where the woodbine grew,
And all the favourite haunts our childhood knew!
How sweet, while all the evil shuns the gaze,
To view the unclouded skies of former days!
  Beloved age of innocence and smiles,
When each wing'd hour some new delight beguiles.
When the gay heart, to life's sweet dayspring true,
Still finds some insect pleasure to pursue.
Bless'd Childhood, hail! — Thee simply will I sing,
And from myself the artless picture bring;
These long-lost scenes to me the past restore,
Each humble friend, each pleasure now no more,
And every stump familiar to my sight
Recalls some fond idea of delight.
  This shrubby knoll was once my favourite seat;
Here did I love at evening to retreat,
And muse alone, till in the vault of night,
Hesper, aspiring, show'd his golden light.
Here once again, remote from human noise,
I sit me down to think of former joys;
Pause on each scene, each treasured scene, once more,
And once again each infant walk explore,
While as each grove and lawn I recognize,
My melted soul suffuses in my eyes.
  And oh! thou Power, whose myriad trains resort
To distant scenes, and picture them to thought;
Whose mirror, held unto the mourner's eye,
Flings to his soul a borrow'd gleam of joy;
Bless'd Memory, guide, with finger nicely true,
Back to my youth my retrospective view;

Recall with faithful vigour to my mind
Each face familiar, each relation kind;
And all the finer traits of them afford,
Whose general outline in my heart is stored.
In yonder cot, along whose mouldering walls
In many a fold the mantling woodbine falls,
The village matron kept her little school,
Gentle of heart, yet knowing well to rule;
Staid was the dame, and modest was her mien;
Her garb was coarse, yet whole, and nicely clean;
Her neatly border'd cap, as lily fair,
Beneath her chin was pinn'd with decent care;
And pendent ruffles, of the whitest lawn,
Of ancient make, her elbows did adorn.
Faint with old age, and dim were grown her eyes,
A pair of spectacles their want supplies;
These does she guard secure, in leathern case,
From thoughtless wights, in some unweeted place.
Here first I enter'd, though with toil and pain,
The low vestibule of learning's fane;
Enter'd with pain, yet soon I found the way,
Though sometimes toilsome, many a sweet display.
Much did I grieve on that ill fated morn
When I was first to school reluctant borne;
Severe I thought the dame, though oft she tried
To soothe my swelling spirits when I sigh'd;
And oft, when harshly she reproved, I wept,
To my lone corner broken-hearted crept,
And thought of tender home, where anger never kept.
But soon inured to alphabetic toils,
Alert I met the dame with jocund smiles;

First at the form, my task for ever true,
A little favourite rapidly I grew:
And oft she stroked my head with fond delight,
Held me a pattern to the dunce's sight;
And as she gave my diligence its praise,
Talk'd of the honours of my future days.
Oh! had the venerable matron thought
Of all the ills by talent often brought;
Could she have seen me when revolving years
Had brought me deeper in the vale of tears,
Then had she wept, and wish'd my wayward fate
Had been a lowlier, an unletter'd state;
Wish'd that, remote from worldly woes and strife,
Unknown, unheard, I might have pass'd through life.
Where in the busy scene, by peace unbless'd,
Shall the poor wanderer find a place of rest?
A lonely mariner on the stormy main,
Without a hope the calms of peace to gain;
Long toss'd by tempests o'er the world's wide shore,
When shall his spirit rest to toil no more?
Not till the light foam of the sea shall lave
The sandy surface of his unwept grave.
Childhood, to thee I turn, from life's alarms,
Serenest season of perpetual calms, —
Turn with delight, and bid the passions cease, —
And joy to think with thee I tasted peace.
Sweet reign of innocence, when no crime defiles,
But each new object brings attendant smiles;
When future evils never haunt the sight,
But all is pregnant with unmix'd delight;

To thee I turn from riot and from noise,
Turn to partake of more congenial joys.
'Neath yonder elm, that stands upon the moor,
When the clock spoke the hour of labour o'er,
What clamorous throngs, what happy groups were
In various postures scattering o'er the green! [seen,
Some shoot the marble, others join the chase
Of self-made stag, or run the emulous race;
While others, seated on the dappled grass,
With doleful tales the light-wing'd minutes pass.
Well I remember how, with gesture starch'd,
A band of soldiers oft with pride we march'd;
For banners to a tall ash we did bind
Our handkerchiefs, flapping to the whistling wind;
And for our warlike arms we sought the mead,
And guns and spears we made of brittle reed;
Then, in uncouth array, our feats to crown,
We storm'd some ruin'd pigsty for a town.
Pleased with our gay disports, the dame was wont
To set her wheel before the cottage front,
And o'er her spectacles would often peer,
To view our gambols, and our boyish gear.
Still as she look'd, her wheel kept turning round,
With its beloved monotony of sound.
When tired with play, we'd set us by her side
(For out of school she never knew to chide),
And wonder at her skill — well known to fame —
For who could match in spinning with the dame?
Her sheets, her linen, which she show'd with pride
To strangers, still her thriftness testified;

Though we poor wights did wonder much, in troth,
How 't was her spinning manufactured cloth.
  Oft would we leave, though well beloved, our play
To chat at home the vacant hour away.
Many 's the time I' ve scamper'd in the glade,
To ask the promised ditty from the maid,
Which well she loved, as well she knew to sing,
While we around her form'd a little ring:
She told of innocence foredoom'd to bleed,
Of wicked guardians bent on bloody deed,
Or little children murder'd as they slept;
While at each pause we wrung our hands and wept.
Sad was such tale, and wonder much did we
Such hearts of stone there in the world could be.
Poor simple wights, ah! little did we ween
The ills that wait on man in life's sad scene!
Ah, little thought that we ourselves should know
This world 's a world of weeping and of woe!
  Beloved moment! then 't was first I caught
The first foundation of romantic thought!
Then first I shed bold Fancy's thrilling tear,
Then first that poesy charm'd mine infant ear.
Soon stored with much of legendary lore,
The sports of childhood charm'd my soul no more.
Far from the scene of gaiety and noise,
Far, far from turbulent and empty joys,
I hied me to the thick o'erarching shade,
And there, on mossy carpet, listless laid,
While at my feet the rippling runnel ran,
The days of wild romance antique I 'd scan;

Soar on the wings of fancy through the air,
To realms of light, and pierce the radiance there.

. . . . . . . . . . .

## PART II.

There are who think that Childhood does not share
With age the cup, the bitter cup, of care:
Alas! they know not this unhappy truth,
That every age, and rank, is born to ruth.
From the first dawn of reason in the mind,
Man is foredoom'd the thorns of grief to find;
At every step has farther cause to know
The draught of pleasure still is dash'd with woe.
Yet in the youthful breast, for ever caught
With some new object for romantic thought,
The impression of the moment quickly flies,
And with the morrow every sorrow dies.
How different manhood!—then does Thought's control
Sink every pang still deeper in the soul;
Then keen Affliction's sad unceasing smart
Becomes a painful resident in the heart;
And care, whom not the gayest can outbrave,
Pursues its feeble victim to the grave.
Then, as each long known friend is summon'd hence,
We feel a void no joy can recompense,
And as we weep o'er every new-made tomb,
Wish that ourselves the next may meet our doom.
Yes, Childhood, thee no rankling woes pursue,
No forms of future ill salute thy view,

No pangs repentant bid thee wake to weep,
But halcyon peace protects thy downy sleep,
And sanguine Hope, through every storm of life,
Shoots her bright beams, and calms the internal strife.
Yet e'en round childhood's heart, a thoughtless shrine,
Affection's little thread will ever twine;
And though but frail may seem each tender tie,
The soul foregoes them but with many a sigh.
Thus, when the long expected moment came,
When forced to leave the gentle-hearted dame,
Reluctant throbbings rose within my breast,
And a still tear my silent grief express'd.
When to the public school compell'd to go,
What novel scenes did on my senses flow?
There in each breast each active power dilates,
Which 'broils whole nations, and convulses states;
Their reigns, by turns alternate, love and hate,
Ambition burns, and factious rebels prate;
And in a smaller range, a smaller sphere,
The dark deformities of man appear.
Yet there the gentler virtues kindred claim,
There Friendship lights her pure untainted flame,
There mild Benevolence delights to dwell,
And sweet Contentment rests without her cell;
And there, 'mid many a stormy soul, we find
The good of heart, the intelligent of mind.
'T was there, O George! with thee I learn'd to join
In Friendship's bands — in amity divine.
Oh, mournful thought! — Where is thy spirit now?
As here I sit on favourite Logar's brow,

And trace below each well remember'd glade,
Where arm in arm, erewhile with thee I stray'd.
Where art thou laid — on what untrodden shore,
Where nought is heard save ocean's sullen roar?
Dost thou in lowly, unlamented state,
At last repose from all the storms of fate?
Methinks I see thee struggling with the wave,
Without one aiding hand stretch'd out to save;
See thee convulsed, thy looks to heaven bend,
And send thy parting sigh unto thy friend:
Or where immeasurable wilds dismay,
Forlorn and sad thou bend'st thy weary way,
While sorrow and disease, with anguish rife,
Consume apace the ebbing springs of life.
Again I see his door against thee shut,
The unfeeling native turn thee from his hut;
I see thee, spent with toil and worn with grief,
Sit on the grass, and wish the long'd relief;
Then lie thee down, the stormy struggle o'er,
Think on thy native land — and rise no more!
  Oh! that thou couldst, from thine august abode,
Survey thy friend in life's dismaying road,
That thou couldst see him, at this moment here,
Embalm thy memory with a pious tear,
And hover o'er him as he gazes round,
Where all the scenes of infant joys surround.
  Yes! yes! his spirit's near! — The whispering
Conveys his voice sad sighing on the trees; [breeze
And lo! his form transparent I perceive,
Borne on the gray mist of the sullen eve:

He hovers near, clad in the night's dim robe,
While deathly silence reigns upon the globe.
Yet ah! whence comes this visionary scene?
'Tis Fancy's wild aërial dream I ween:
By her inspired, when reason takes its flight,
What fond illusions beam upon the sight!
She waves her hand, and lo! what forms appear!
What magic sounds salute the wondering ear!
Once more o'er distant regions do we tread,
And the cold grave yields up its cherish'd dead;
While, present sorrows banish'd far away,
Unclouded azure gilds the placid day,
Or, in the future's cloud-encircled face,
Fair scenes of bliss to come we fondly trace,
And draw minutely every little wile,
Which shall the feathery hours of time beguile.
So when forlorn, and lonesome at her gate,
The Royal Mary solitary sate,
And view'd the moonbeam trembling on the wave,
And heard the hollow surge her prison lave,
Towards France's distant coast she bent her sight,
For there her soul had wing'd its longing flight;
There did she form full many a scheme of joy,
Visions of bliss unclouded with alloy,
Which bright thro' Hope's deceitful optics beam'd,
And all became the surety which it seem'd;
She wept, yet felt, while all within was calm,
In every tear a melancholy charm.
To yonder hill, whose sides, deform'd and steep,
Just yield a scanty sustenance to the sheep,

With thee, my friend, I oftentimes have sped,
To see the sun rise from his healthy bed;
To watch the aspect of the summer morn,
Smiling upon the golden fields of corn,
And taste, delighted, of superior joys,
Beheld through sympathy's enchanted eyes:
With silent admiration oft we view'd
The myriad hues o'er heaven's blue concave strew'd;
The fleecy clouds, of every tint and shade,
Round which the silvery sunbeam glancing play'd,
And the round orb itself, in azure throne,
Just peeping o'er the blue hill's ridgy zone;
We mark'd delighted, how with aspect gay,
Reviving Nature hail'd returning day;
Mark'd how the flowerets rear'd their drooping heads,
And the wild lambkins bounded o'er the meads,
While from each tree, in tones of sweet delight,
The birds sung pæans to the source of light:
Oft have we watch'd the speckled lark arise,
Leave his grass bed, and soar to kindred skies,
And rise, and rise, till the pain'd sight no more
Could trace him in his high aërial tour;
Though on the ear, at intervals, his song
Came wafted slow the wavy breeze along;
And we have thought how happy were our lot,
Bless'd with some sweet, some solitary cot,
Where, from the peep of day, till russet eve
Began in every dell her forms to weave,
We might pursue our sports from day to day,
And in each other's arms wear life away.

At sultry noon too, when our toils were done,
We to the gloomy glen were wont to run;
There on the turf we lay, while at our feet
The cooling rivulet rippled softly sweet;
And mused on holy theme, and ancient lore,
Of deeds, and days, and heroes now no more;
Heard, as his solemn harp Isaiah swept,
Sung woe unto the wicked land — and wept;
Or, fancy-led, saw Jeremiah mourn
In solemn sorrow o'er Judea's urn.
Then to another shore perhaps would rove,
With Plato talk in his Ilyssian grove;
Or, wandering where the Thespian palace rose,
Weep once again o'er fair Jocasta's woes.
Sweet then to us was that romantic band,
The ancient legends of our native land —
Chivalric Britomart, and Una fair,
And courteous Constance, doom'd to dark despair,
By turns our thoughts engaged; and oft we talk'd
Of times when monarch superstition stalk'd,
And when the blood-fraught galliots of Rome
Brought the grand Druid fabric to its doom:
While, where the wood-hung Meinai's waters flow,
The hoary harpers pour'd the strain of woe.
While thus employ'd, to us how sad the bell
Which summon'd us to school! 'T was Fancy's knell,
And, sadly sounding on the sullen ear,
It spoke of study pale, and chilling fear.
Yet even then, (for oh! what chains can bind,
What powers control, the energies of mind!)

E'en then we soar'd to many a height sublime,
And many a day-dream charm'd the lazy time.
At evening too, how pleasing was our walk,
Endear'd by Friendship's unrestrained talk,
When to the upland heights we bent our way,
To view the last beam of departing day;
How calm was all around! no playful breeze
Sigh'd 'mid the wavy foliage of the trees,
But all was still, save when, with drowsy song,
The gray-fly wound his sullen horn along;
And save when, heard in soft, yet merry glee,
The distant church bells' mellow harmony;
The silver mirror of the lucid brook,
That 'mid the tufted broom its still course took;
The rugged arch, that clasp'd its silent tides,
With moss and rank weeds hanging down its sides;
The craggy rock, that jutted on the sight;
The shrieking bat, that took its heavy flight;
All, all was pregnant with divine delight.
We loved to watch the swallow swimming high,
In the bright azure of the vaulted sky;
Or gaze upon the clouds, whose colour'd pride
Was scatter'd thinly o'er the welkin wide,
And tinged with such variety of shade,
To the charm'd soul sublimest thoughts convey'd.
In these what forms romantic did we trace,
While Fancy led us o'er the realms of space!
Now we espied the Thunderer in his car,
Leading the embattled seraphim to war,

Then stately towers descried, sublimely high,
In Gothic grandeur frowning on the sky—
Or saw, wide stretching o'er the azure height,
A ridge of glaciers in mural white,
Hugely terrific.—But those times are o'er,
And the fond scene can charm mine eyes no more;
For thou art gone, and I am left below,
Alone to struggle through this world of woe.
The scene is o'er—still seasons onward roll,
And each revolve conducts me toward the goal;
Yet all is blank, without one soft relief,
One endless continuity of grief;
And the tired soul, now led to thoughts sublime,
Looks but for rest beyond the bounds of time.
Toil on, toil on, ye busy crowds, that pant
For hoards of wealth which ye will never want:
And lost to all but gain, with ease resign
The calms of peace and happiness divine!
Far other cares be mine—Men little crave
In this short journey to the silent grave;
And the poor peasant, bless'd with peace and health,
I envy more than Crœsus with his wealth.
Yet grieve not I, that Fate did not decree
Paternal acres to await on me;
She gave me more, she placed within my breast
A heart with little pleased—with little bless'd:
I look around me, where, on every side,
Extensive manors spread in wealthy pride;
And could my sight be borne to either zone,
I should not find one foot of land my own.

But whither do I wander? shall the muse,
For golden baits, her simple theme refuse?
Oh, no! but while the weary spirit greets
The fading scenes of childhood's far gone sweets,
It catches all the infant's wandering tongue,
And prattles on in desultory song.
That song must close — the gloomy mists of night
Obscure the pale stars' visionary light,
And ebon darkness, clad in vapoury wet,
Steals on the welkin in primæval jet.
The song must close. — Once more my adverse lot
Leads me reluctant from this cherish'd spot:
Again compels to plunge in busy life,
And brave the hatcful turbulence of strife.
Scenes of my youth — ere my unwilling feet
Are turn'd for ever from this loved retreat,
Ere on these fields, with plenty cover'd o'er,
My eyes are closed to ope on them no more,
Let me ejaculate, to feeling due,
One long, one last affectionate adieu.
Grant that, if ever Providence should please
To give me an old age of peace and ease,
Grant that, in these sequester'd shades, my days
May wear away in gradual decays:
And oh! ye spirits, who unbodied play,
Unseen upon the pinions of the day,
Kind genii of my native fields benign,
Who were . . . . . . . .

# THE CHRISTIAD.

## A DIVINE POEM.

## BOOK I.

I.

I SING the Cross! — Ye white-robed angel choirs,
Who know the chords of harmony to sweep,
Ye who o'er holy David's varying wires
Were wont, of old, your hovering watch to keep,
Oh, now descend! and with your harpings deep,
Pouring sublime the full symphonious stream
Of music, such as soothes the saint's last sleep,
Awake my slumbering spirit from its dream,
And teach me how to exalt the high mysterious theme.

II.

Mourn! Salem, mourn! low lies thine humbled state,
Thy glittering fanes are level'd with the ground!
Fallen is thy pride! — Thine halls are desolate!
Where erst was heard the timbrels' sprightly sound,
And frolic pleasures tripp'd the nightly round,
There breeds the wild fox lonely, — and aghast
Stands the mute pilgrim at the void profound,
Unbroke by noise, save when the hurrying blast
Sighs, like a spirit, deep along the cheerless waste.

III.

It is for this, proud Solyma! thy towers
Lie crumbling in the dust; for this forlorn
Thy genius wails along thy desert bowers,
While stern Destruction laughs, as if in scorn,
That thou didst dare insult God's eldest born;
And, with most bitter persecuting ire,
Pursued his footsteps till the last day dawn
Rose on his fortunes — and thou saw'st the fire
That came to light the world, in one great flash expire.

IV.

Oh! for a pencil dipp'd in living light,
To paint the agonies that Jesus bore!
Oh! for the long lost harp of Jesse's might,
To hymn the Saviour's praise from shore to shore;
While seraph hosts the lofty pæan pour,
And Heaven enraptured lists the loud acclaim!
May a frail mortal dare the theme explore?
May he to human ears his weak song frame?
Oh! may he dare to sing Messiah's glorious name.

V.

Spirits of pity! mild crusaders, come!
Buoyant on clouds around your minstrel float,
And give him eloquence who else were dumb,
And raise to feeling and to fire his note!
And thou, Urania! who dost still devote
Thy nights and days to God's eternal shrine,
Whose mild eyes 'lumined what Isaiah wrote,

Throw o'er thy Bard that solemn stole of thine,
And clothe him for the fight with energy divine.

VI.

When from the temple's lofty summit prone,
Satan, o'ercome, fell down; and 'throned there,
The son of God confess'd in splendour shone:
Swift as the glancing sunbeam cuts the air,
Mad with defeat, and yelling his despair,

. . . . . . . . . .

Fled the stern king of Hell—and with the glare
Of gliding meteors, ominous and red,
Shot athwart the clouds that gather'd round his head.

VII.

Right o'er the Euxine, and that gulf which late
The rude Massagetæ adored, he bent
His northering course, while round, in dusky state
The assembling fiends their summon'd troops augment;
Clothed in dark mists, upon their way they went,
While as they pass'd to regions more severe,
The Lapland sorcerer swell'd with loud lament
The solitary gale; and, fill'd with fear,
The howling dogs bespoke unholy spirits near.

VIII.

Where the North Pole, in moody solitude,
Spreads her huge tracks and frozen wastes around,
There ice-rocks piled aloft, in order rude,
Form a gigantic hall, where never sound

Startled dull Silence' ear, save when profound
The smoke-frost mutter'd: there drear Cold for aye [mound,
Thrones him, — and, fix'd on his primæval
Ruin, the giant, sits; while stern Dismay
Stalks like some woe-struck man along the desert way.

IX.

In that drear spot, grim Desolation's lair,
No sweet remain of life encheers the sight;
The dancing heart's blood in an instant there
Would freeze to marble. — Mingling day and night [light)
(Sweet interchange, which makes our labours
Are there unknown; while in the summer skies
The sun rolls ceaseless round his heavenly height,
Nor ever sets till from the scene he flies, [rise.
And leaves the long bleak night of half the year to

X.

'T was there, yet shuddering from the burning lake,
Satan had fix'd their next consistory,
When parting last he fondly hoped to shake
Messiah's constancy, — and thus to free
The powers of darkness from the dread decree
Of bondage brought by him, and circumvent
The unerring ways of Him whose eye can see
The womb of Time, and, in its embryo pent,
Discern the colours clear of every dark event.

XI.

Here the stern monarch stay'd his rapid flight,
And his thick hosts, as with a jetty pall,
Hovering obscured the north star's peaceful light,
Waiting on wing their haughty chieftain's call.
He, meanwhile, downward, with a sullen fall,
Dropp'd on the echoing ice. Instant the sound
Of their broad vans was hush'd, and o'er the hall,
Vast and obscure, the gloomy cohorts bound,
Till, wedged in ranks, the seat of Satan they surround.

XII.

High on a solium of the solid wave,
Prank'd with rude shapes by the fantastic frost,
He stood in silence ; — now keen thoughts engrave
Dark figures on his front; and, tempest-toss'd,
He fears to say that every hope is lost.
Meanwhile the multitude as death are mute;
So, ere the tempest on Malacca's coast,
Sweet Quiet, gently touching her soft lute,
Sings to the whispering waves the prelude to dispute.

XIII.

At length collected, o'er the dark Divan
The arch fiend glanced as by the Boreal blaze
Their downcast brows were seen, and thus began
His fierce harangue: — "Spirits! our better days
Are now elapsed; Moloch and Belial's praise

Shall sound no more in groves by myriads trod.
Lo! the light breaks; — The astonish'd nations gaze,
For us is lifted high the avenging rod!
For, spirits! this is He, — this is the Son of God!

XIV.

"What then! — shall Satan's spirit crouch to fear?
Shall he who shook the pillars of God's reign
Drop from his unnerved arm the hostile spear?
Madness! The very thought would make me fain
To tear the spanglets from yon gaudy plain,
And hurl them at their Maker! — Fix'd as Fate
I am his foe! — Yea, though his pride should deign
To soothe mine ire with half his regal state,
Still would I burn with fix'd unalterable hate.

XV.

"Now hear the issue of my cursed emprize.
When from our last sad synod I took flight,
Buoyed with false hopes, in some deep-laid disguise,
To tempt this vaunted Holy One to write
His own self-condemnation; in the plight
Of aged man in the lone wilderness,
Gathering a few stray sticks, I met his sight;
And, leaning on my staff, seem'd much to guess
What cause could mortal bring to that forlorn recess.

XVI.

"Then thus in homely guise I featly framed
My lowly speech:—"Good Sir, what leads this way [blamed
Your wandering steps? must hapless chance be
That you so far from haunt of mortals stray?
Here have I dwelt for many a lingering day,
Nor trace of man have seen: but how! methought
Thou wert the youth on whom God's holy ray
I saw descend in Jordan, when John taught
That he to fallen man the saving promise brought.'

XVII.

"'I am that man,' said Jesus, 'I am He. [feet
But truce to questions—Canst thou point my
To some low hut, if haply such there be
In this wild labyrinth, where I may meet
With homely greeting, and may sit and eat;
For forty days I have tarried fasting here,
Hid in the dark glens of this lone retreat,
And now I hunger; and my fainting ear [near.'
Longs much to greet the sound of fountains gushing

XVIII.

"Then thus I answer'd wily:—'If, indeed,
Son of our God thou be'st, what need to seek
For food from men?—Lo! on these flint stones feed,
Bid them be bread! Open thy lips and speak,

And living rills from yon parch'd rock will break.'
Instant as I had spoke, his piercing eye
Fix'd on my face; — the blood forsook my cheek,
I could not bear his gaze; — my mask slipp'd by;
I would have shunn'd his look, but had not power to fly.

XIX.

"Then he rebuked me with the holy word —
Accursed sounds; but now my native pride
Return'd, and by no foolish qualm deterr'd,
I bore him from the mountain's woody side
Up to the summit, where extending wide
Kingdoms and cities, palaces and fanes,
Bright sparkling in the sunbeams, were descried,
And in gay dance, amid luxuriant plains,
Tripp'd to the jocund reed the emasculated swains.

XX.

"'Behold,' I cried, 'these glories! scenes divine!
Thou whose sad prime in pining want decays;
And these, O rapture! these shall all be thine,
If thou wilt give to me, not God, the praise.
Hath he not given to indigence thy days?
Is not thy portion peril here and pain?
Oh! leave his temples, shun his wounding ways!
Seize the tiara! these mean weeds disdain,
Kneel, kneel, thou man of woe, and peace and splendour gain.'

XXI.

"'Is it not written,' sternly he replied,
'Tempt not the Lord thy God!' Frowning he spake,
And instant sounds, as of the ocean tide,
Rose, and the whirlwind from its prison brake,
And caught me up aloft, till in one flake
The sidelong volley met my swift career,
And smote me earthward.—Jove himself might quake
At such a fall; my sinews crack'd, and near,
Obscure and dizzy sounds seem'd ringing in mine ear.

XXII.

"Senseless and stunn'd I lay; till casting round
My half unconscious gaze, I saw the foe
Borne on a car of roses to the ground,
By volant angels; and as sailing slow
He sunk the hoary battlement below,
While on the tall spire slept the slant sunbeam,
Sweet on the enamour'd zephyr was the flow
Of heavenly instruments. Such strains oft seem,
On star-light hill, to soothe the Syrian shepherd's dream.

XXIII.

"I saw blaspheming. Hate renew'd my strength;
I smote the ether with my iron wing,
And left the accursed scene.— Arrived at length
In these drear halls, to ye, my peers! I bring
The tidings of defeat. Hell's haughty king

Thrice vanquish'd, baffled, smitten, and dismay'd!
O shame! Is this the hero who could fling
Defiance at his Maker, while array'd,
High o'er the walls of light, rebellion's banners play'd!

XXIV.

"Yet shall not Heaven's bland minions triumph long;
Hell yet shall have revenge. O glorious sight,
Prophetic visions on my fancy throng,
I see wild Agony's lean finger write
Sad figures on his forehead! — Keenly bright
Revenge's flambeau burns! Now in his eyes
Stand the hot tears, — immantled in the night,
Lo! he retires to mourn! — I hear his cries!
He faints — he falls — and lo! — 't is true, ye powers, he dies."

XXV.

Thus spake the chieftain, — and as if he view'd
The scene he pictured, with his foot advanced
And chest inflated, motionless he stood,
While under his uplifted shield he glanced,
With straining eyeball fix'd, like one entranced,
On viewless air; — thither the dark platoon
Gazed wondering, nothing seen, save when there danced
The northern flash, or fiend late fled from noon,
Darken'd the disk of the descending moon.

XXVI.

Silence crept stilly through the ranks.—The breeze
Spake most distinctly. As the sailor stands,
When all the midnight gasping from the seas
Break boding sobs, and to his sight expands
High on the shrouds the spirit that commands
The ocean-farer's life; so stiff—so sear
Stood each dark power;—while through their numerous bands
Beat not one heart, and mingling hope and fear
Now told them all was lost, now bade revenge appear.

XXVII.

One there was there, whose loud defying tongue
Nor hope nor fear had silenced, but the swell
Of over-boiling malice. Utterance long
His passion mock'd, and long he strove to tell
His labouring ire; still syllable none fell
From his pale quivering lip, but died away
For very fury; from each hollow cell
Half sprang his eyes, that cast a flamy ray,
And . . . . . . . . . . . . .

XXVIII.

"This comes," at length burst from the furious chief,
"This comes of distant counsels! Here behold
The fruits of wily cunning! the relief
Which coward policy would fain unfold,

To soothe the powers that warr'd with Heaven
of old!
O wise! O potent! O sagacious snare!
And lo! our prince — the mighty and the bold,
There stands he, spell-struck, gaping at the air,
While Heaven subverts his reign, and plants her
standard there."

XXIX.

Here, as recover'd, Satan fix'd his eye
Full on the speaker; dark it was and stern;
He wrapp'd his black vest round him gloomily,
And stood like one whom weightiest thoughts
concern.
Him Moloch mark'd, and strove again to turn
His soul to rage. "Behold, behold," he cried,
"The lord of Hell, who made these legions
spurn
Almighty rule — behold he lays aside [fied."
The spear of just revenge, and shrinks, by man de-

XXX.

Thus ended Moloch, and his burning tongue
Hung quivering, as if [mad] to quench its heat
In slaughter. So, his native wilds among,
The famish'd tiger pants, when, near his seat,
Press'd on the sands, he marks the traveller's
feet.
Instant low murmurs rose, and many a sword

Had from its scabbard sprung; but toward the seat
Of the arch-fiend all turn'd with one accord,
As loud he thus harangued the sanguinary horde.

. . . . . . .

"Ye powers of Hell, I am no coward. I proved this of old: who led your forces against the armies of Jehovah? Who coped with Ithuriel and the thunders of the Almighty? Who, when stunned and confused ye lay on the burning lake, who first awoke, and collected your scattered powers? Lastly, who led you across the unfathomable abyss to this delightful world, and established that reign here which now totters to its base? How, therefore, dares yon treacherous fiend to cast a stain on Satan's bravery? he who preys only on the defenceless—who sucks the blood of infants, and delights only in acts of ignoble cruelty and unequal contention. Away with the boaster who never joins in action, but, like a cormorant, hovers over the field, to feed upon the wounded, and overwhelm the dying. True bravery is as remote from rashness as from hesitation; let us counsel coolly, but let us execute our counselled purposes determinately. In power we have learned, by that experiment which lost us Heaven, that we are inferior to the Thunder-bearer:—In subtlety, in subtlety alone we are his equals. Open war is impossible.

. . . . . . .

"Thus we shall pierce our conqueror through the race
Which as himself he loves; thus if we fall,
We fall not with the anguish, the disgrace,
Of falling unrevenged. The stirring call
Of vengeance rings within me! Warriors all,
The word is vengeance, and the spur despair.
Away with coward wiles! — Death's coal-black pall
Be now our standard! — Be our torch the glare
Of cities fired! our fifes, the shrieks that fill the air!"

Him answering rose Mecashpim, who of old,
Far in the silence of Chaldea's groves,
Was worshipp'd, God of Fire, with charms untold
And mystery. His wandering spirit roves,
Now vainly searching for the flame it loves;
And sits and mourns like some white-robed sire,
Where stood his temple, and where fragrant cloves
And cinnamon unheap'd the sacred pyre,
And nightly magi watch'd the everlasting fire.

He waved his robe of flame, he cross'd his breast,
And sighing — his papyrus scarf survey'd,
Woven with dark characters, then thus address'd
The troubled council.

. . . . . . . .

I.

Thus far have I pursued my solemn theme
With self-rewarding toil, thus far have sung
Of godlike deeds, far loftier than beseem
The lyre which I in early days have strung:
And now my spirit's faint, and I have hung
The shell, that solaced me in saddest hour,
On the dark cypress! and the strings which rung
With Jesus' praise, their harpings now are o'er,
Or, when the breeze comes by, moan and are heard no more.

And must the harp of Judah sleep again?
Shall I no more reanimate the lay?
Oh! thou who visitest the sons of men,
Thou who dost listen when the humble pray,
One little space prolong my mournful day!
One little lapse suspend thy last decree!
I am a youthful traveller in the way,
And this slight boon would consecrate to thee,
Ere I with Death shake hands, and smile that I am free.

. . . . . . . . .
. . . . . . . . .

## LINES WRITTEN ON A SURVEY OF THE HEAVENS,

### IN THE MORNING BEFORE DAYBREAK.

Ye many twinkling stars, who yet do hold
Your brilliant places in the sable vault
Of night's dominions! — Planets, and central orbs
Of other systems! — big as the burning sun
Which lights this nether globe, — yet to our eye
Small as the glowworm's lamp! — To you I raise
My lowly orisons, while, all bewilder'd,
My vision strays o'er your ethereal hosts;
Too vast, too boundless for our narrow mind,
Warp'd with low prejudices, to unfold,
And sagely comprehend. Thence higher soaring,
Through ye I raise my solemn thoughts to Him,
The mighty Founder of this wondrous maze,
The great Creator! Him! who now sublime,
Wrapt in the solitary amplitude
Of boundless space, above the rolling spheres
Sits on his silent throne and meditates.
The angelic hosts, in their inferior Heaven,
Hymn to the golden harps his praise sublime,
Repeating loud, "The Lord our God is great,"
In varied harmonies. — The glorious sounds
Roll o'er the air serene — The Æolian spheres,
Harping along their viewless boundaries,

Catch the full note, and cry, "The Lord is great,"
Responding to the Seraphim. O'er all
From orb to orb, to the remotest verge
Of the created world, the sound is borne,
Till the whole universe is full of Him.
  Oh! 'tis this heavenly harmony which now
In fancy strikes upon my listening ear,
And thrills my inmost soul. It bids me smile
On the vain world, and all its bustling cares,
And gives a shadowy glimpse of future bliss.
  Oh! what is man, when at ambition's height,
What even are kings, when balanced in the scale
Of these stupendous worlds! Almighty God!
Thou, the dread author of these wondrous works!
Say, canst thou cast on me, poor passing worm,
One look of kind benevolence? — Thou canst:
For Thou art full of universal love,
And in thy boundless goodness wilt impart
Thy beams as well to me as to the proud,
The pageant insects of a glittering hour.
  Oh! when reflecting on these truths sublime,
How insignificant do all the joys,
The gaudes, and honours of the world appear!
How vain ambition! Why has my wakeful lamp
Outwatch'd the slow-paced night! — Why on the page,
The schoolman's labour'd page, have I employ'd
The hours devoted by the world to rest,
And needful to recruit exhausted nature?
Say, can the voice of narrow Fame repay

The loss of health? or can the hope of glory
Lend a new throb into my languid heart,
Cool, even now, my feverish aching brow,
Relume the fires of this deep sunken eye,
Or paint new colours on this pallid cheek?
  Say, foolish one — can that unbodied fame,
For which thou barterest health and happiness,
Say, can it soothe the slumbers of the grave?
Give a new zest to bliss, or chase the pangs
Of everlasting punishment condign?
Alas! how vain are mortal man's desires!
How fruitless his pursuits! Eternal God!
Guide thou my footsteps in the way of truth,
And oh! assist me so to live on earth,
That I may die in peace, and claim a place
In thy high dwelling. — All but this is folly,
The vain illusions of deceitful life.

---

## LINES SUPPOSED TO BE SPOKEN BY A LOVER AT THE GRAVE OF HIS MISTRESS.

OCCASIONED BY A SITUATION IN A ROMANCE.

Mary, the moon is sleeping on thy grave,
And on the turf thy lover sad is kneeling,
The big tear in his eye. — Mary, awake,
From thy dark house arise, and bless his sight
On the pale moonbeam gliding. Soft, and low,
Pour on the silver ear of night thy tale,

Thy whisper'd tale of comfort and of love,
To soothe thy Edward's lorn, distracted soul,
And cheer his breaking heart.— Come, as thou didst,
When o'er the barren moors the night wind howl'd,
And the deep thunders shook the ebon throne
Of the startled night!— O! then, as lone reclining,
I listen'd sadly to the dismal storm,
Thou on the lambent lightnings wild careering
Didst strike my moody eye;— dead pale thou wert,
Yet passing lovely.— Thou didst smile upon me,
And oh! thy voice it rose so musical,
Betwixt the hollow pauses of the storm,
That at the sound the winds forgot to rave,
And the stern demon of the tempest, charm'd,
Sunk on his rocking throne to still repose,
Lock'd in the arms of silence.
Spirit of her!
My only love! O! now again arise,
And let once more thine aëry accents fall
Soft on my listening ear. The night is calm,
The gloomy willows wave in sinking cadence
With the stream that sweeps below. Divinely swelling
On the still air, the distant waterfall
Mingles its melody;— and, high above,
The pensive empress of the solemn night,
Fitful, emerging from the rapid clouds,
Shows her chaste face in the meridian sky.
No wicked elves upon the Warlock-knoll
Dare now assemble at their mystic revels.

It is a night when, from their primrose beds,
The gentle ghosts of injured innocents
Are known to rise and wander on the breeze,
Or take their stand by the oppressor's couch,
And strike grim terror to his guilty soul.
The spirit of my love might now awake,
And hold its custom'd converse.
Mary, lo!
Thy Edward kneels upon thy verdant grave,
And calls upon thy name. The breeze that blows
On his wan cheek will soon sweep over him
In solemn music a funereal dirge,
Wild and most sorrowful. His cheek is pale,
The worm that prey'd upon thy youthful bloom
It canker'd green on his. Now lost he stands,
The ghost of what he was, and the cold dew,
Which bathes his aching temples, gives sure omen
Of speedy dissolution. Mary, soon
Thy love will lay his pallid cheek to thine,
And sweetly will he sleep with thee in death.

---

## MY STUDY.

### A LETTER IN HUDIBRASTIC VERSE.

You bid me, Ned, describe the place
Where I, one of the rhyming race,
Pursue my studies con amore,
And wanton with the muse in glory.

Well, figure to your senses straight,
Upon the house's topmost height,
A closet just six feet by four,
With whitewash'd walls and plaster floor.
So noble large, 't is scarcely able
To admit a single chair and table:
And (lest the muse should die with cold)
A smoky grate my fire to hold:
So wondrous small, 't would much it pose
To melt the icedrop on one's nose;
And yet so big, it covers o'er
Full half the spacious room and more.
A window vainly stuff'd about,
To keep November's breezes out,
So crazy, that the panes proclaim
That soon they mean to leave the frame.
My furniture I sure may crack —
A broken chair without a back;
A table wanting just two legs,
One end sustain'd by wooden pegs;
A desk — of that I am not fervent,
The work of, Sir, your humble servant;
(Who, though I say 't, am no such fumbler;)
A glass decanter and a tumbler,
From which my night-parch'd throat I lave,
Luxurious, with the limpid wave.
A chest of drawers, in antique sections,
And saw'd by me in all directions;
So small, Sir, that whoever views 'em
Swears nothing but a doll could use 'em.

To these, if you will add a store
Of oddities upon the floor,
A pair of globes, electric balls,
Scales, quadrants, prisms, and cobbler's awls,
And crowds of books, on rotten shelves,
Octavos, folios, quartos, twelves;
I think, dear Ned, you curious dog,
You 'll have my earthly catalogue.
But stay, — I nearly had left out
My bellows destitute of snout;
And on the walls, — Good Heavens! why there
I 've such a load of precious ware,
Of heads, and coins, and silver medals,
And organ works, and broken pedals;
(For I was once a-building music,
Though soon of that employ I grew sick);
And skeletons of laws which shoot
All out of one primordial root;
That you, at such a sight, would swear
Confusion's self had settled there.
There stands, just by a broken sphere,
A Cicero without an ear,
A neck, on which, by logic good,
I know for sure a head once stood;
But who it was the able master
Had moulded in the mimic plaster,
Whether 't was Pope, or Coke, or Burn,
I never yet could justly learn:
But knowing well, that any head
Is made to answer for the dead,

(And sculptors first their faces frame,
And after pitch upon a name,
Nor think it aught of a misnomer
To christen Chaucer's busto Homer, [know,
Because they both have beards, which, you
Will mark them well from Joan, and Juno,)
For some great man, I could not tell
But Neck might answer just as well,
So perch'd it up, all in a row
With Chatham and with Cicero.
  Then all around, in just degree,
A range of portraits you may see,
Of mighty men and eke of women,
Who are no whit inferior to men.
  With these fair dames, and heroes round,
I call my garret classic ground.
For though confined, 't will well contain
The ideal flights of Madam Brain.
No dungeon's walls, no cell confined
Can cramp the energies of mind!
Thus, though my heart may seem so small,
I 've friends, and 't will contain them all;
And should it e'er become so cold
That these it will no longer hold,
No more may Heaven her blessings give,
I shall not then be fit to live.

## DESCRIPTION OF A SUMMER'S EVE.

Down the sultry arc of day
The burning wheels have urged their way;
And eve along the western skies
Sheds her intermingling dyes.
Down the deep, the miry lane,
Creaking comes the empty wain,
And driver on the shaft-horse sits,
Whistling now and then by fits:
And oft, with his accustom'd call,
Urging on the sluggish Ball.
The barn is still, the master 's gone,
And thresher puts his jacket on,
While Dick, upon the ladder tall,
Nails the dead kite to the wall.
Here comes shepherd Jack at last,
He has penn'd the sheepcote fast,
For 't was but two nights before,
A lamb was eaten on the moor:
His empty wallet Rover carries,
Nor for Jack, when near home, tarries.
With lolling tongue he runs to try
If the horse-trough be not dry.
The milk is settled in the pans,
And supper messes in the cans;
In the hovel carts are wheel'd,
And both the colts are drove a-field;

The horses are all bedded up,
And the ewe is with the tup.
The snare for Mister Fox is set,
The leaven laid, the thatching wet,
And Bess has slink'd away to talk
With Roger in the holly walk.
  Now, on the settle all, but Bess,
Are set to eat their supper mess;
And little Tom and roguish Kate
Are swinging on the meadow gate.
Now they chat of various things,
Of taxes, ministers, and kings,
Or else tell all the village news,
How madam did the squire refuse;
How parson on his tithes was bent,
And landlord oft distrain'd for rent.
Thus do they talk, till in the sky
The pale-eyed moon is mounted high,
And from the alehouse drunken Ned
Had reel'd — then hasten all to bed.
The mistress sees that lazy Kate
The happing coal on kitchen grate
Has laid — while master goes throughout,
Sees shutters fast, the mastiff out,
The candles safe, the hearths all clear,
And nought from thieves or fire to fear;
Then both to bed together creep,
And join the general troop of sleep.

## LINES,

Written impromptu, on reading the following passage in Mr. Capel Lofft's beautiful and interesting Preface to Nathaniel Bloomfield's Poems, just published:—"It has a mixture of the sportive, which deepens the impression of its melancholy close. I could have wished, as I have said in a short note, the conclusion had been otherwise. The sours of life less offend my taste than its sweets delight it."

Go to the raging sea, and say, "Be still!"
Bid the wild lawless winds obey thy will;
Preach to the storm, and reason with Despair,
But tell not Misery's son that life is fair.
Thou, who in Plenty's lavish lap hast roll'd,
And every year with new delight hast told,
Thou, who, recumbent on the lacquer'd barge,
Hast dropt down joy's gay stream of pleasant marge,
Thou mayst extol life's calm untroubled sea,
The storms of misery never burst on thee.
Go to the mat, where squalid Want reclines,
Go to the shade obscure, where merit pines;
Abide with him whom Penury's charms control,
And bind the rising yearnings of his soul,
Survey his sleepless couch, and, standing there,
Tell the poor pallid wretch that life is fair!
Press thou the lonely pillow of his head,
And ask why sleep his languid eyes has fled;

Mark his dew'd temples, and his half shut eye,
His trembling nostrils, and his deep drawn sigh,
His muttering mouth contorted with despair,
And ask if Genius could inhabit there.
  Oh, yes! that sunken eye with fire once gleam'd,
And rays of light from its full circlet stream'd:
But now Neglect has stung him to the core,
And Hope's wild raptures thrill his breast no more;
Domestic Anguish winds his vitals round,
And added Grief compels him to the ground.
Lo! o'er his manly form, decay'd and wan,
The shades of death with gradual steps steal on;
And the pale mother, pining to decay,
Weeps for her boy her wretched life away.
  Go, child of Fortune! to his early grave,
Where o'er his head obscure the rank weeds wave;
Behold the heart-wrung parent lay her head
On the cold turf, and ask to share his bed.
Go, child of Fortune, take thy lesson there,
And tell us then that life is wondrous fair!
  Yet, Lofft, in thee, whose hand is still stretch'd forth,
To encourage genius, and to foster worth;
On thee, the unhappy's firm, unfailing friend,
'T is just that every blessing should descend;
'T is just that life to thee should only show
Her fairer side but little mix'd with woe.

## WRITTEN IN THE PROSPECT OF DEATH.

Sad solitary Thought, who keep'st thy vigils,
Thy solemn vigils, in the sick man's mind;
Communing lonely with his sinking soul,
And musing on the dubious glooms that lie
In dim obscurity before him, — thee,
Wrapt in thy dark magnificence, I call
At this still midnight hour, this awful season,
When, on my bed, in wakeful restlessness,
I turn me wearisome; while all around,
All, all, save me, sink in forgetfulness;
I only wake to watch the sickly taper
Which lights me to my tomb. Yes, 'tis the hand
Of death I feel press heavy on my vitals,
Slow sapping the warm current of existence.
My moments now are few — the sand of life
Ebbs fastly to its finish. Yet a little,
And the last fleeting particle will fall
Silent, unseen, unnoticed, unlamented.
Come then, sad Thought, and let us meditate,
While meditate we may. — We have now
But a small portion of what men call time
To hold communion; for even now the knife,
The separating knife, I feel divide
The tender bond that binds my soul to earth.
Yes, I must die — I feel that I must die;
And though to me has life been dark and dreary,
Though Hope for me has smiled but to deceive,

And Disappointment still pursued her blandishments,
Yet do I feel my soul recoil within me
As I contemplate the dim gulf of death,
The shuddering void, the awful blank — futurity.
Ay, I had plann'd full many a sanguine scheme
Of earthly happiness — romantic schemes,
And fraught with loveliness; and it is hard
To feel the hand of Death arrest one's steps,
Throw a chill blight o'er all one's budding hopes,
And hurl one's soul untimely to the shades,
Lost in the gaping gulf of blank oblivion.
Fifty years hence, and who will hear of Henry?
Oh! none; — another busy brood of beings
Will shoot up in the interim, and none
Will hold him in remembrance. I shall sink
As sinks a stranger in the crowded streets
Of busy London: — Some short bustle's caused,
A few inquiries, and the crowds close in,
And all's forgotten. — On my grassy grave
The men of future times will careless tread,
And read my name upon the sculptured stone;
Nor will the sound, familiar to their ears,
Recall my vanish'd memory. I did hope
For better things! — I hoped I should not leave
The earth without a vestige; — Fate decrees
It shall be otherwise, and I submit.
Henceforth, oh, world, no more of thy desires!
No more of hope! the wanton vagrant Hope!
I abjure all. Now other cares engross me,
And my tired soul, with emulative haste,
Looks to its God, and prunes its wings for heaven.

## VERSES.

When pride and envy, and the scorn
  Of wealth my heart with gall imbued,
I thought how pleasant were the morn
  Of silence, in the solitude;
To hear the forest bee on wing;
Or by the stream, or woodland spring,
To lie and muse alone — alone,
While the tinkling waters moan,
Or such wild sounds arise, as say,
Man and noise are far away.

Now, surely, thought I, there 's enow
  To fill life's dusty way;
And who will miss a poet's feet,
  Or wonder where he stray:
So to the woods and wastes I'll go,
  And I will build an osier bower,
And sweetly there to me shall flow
  The meditative hour.

And when the Autumn's withering hand,
Shall strew with leaves the sylvan land,
I'll to the forest caverns hie:
And in the dark and stormy nights
I'll listen to the shrieking sprites,
Who, in the wintry wolds and floods,
Keep jubilee, and shred the woods;
Or, as it drifted soft and slow,
Hurl in ten thousand shapes the snow.

. . . . . . . . .

## FRAGMENT.

Oh! thou most fatal of Pandora's train,
  Consumption! silent cheater of the eye;
Thou comest not robed in agonizing pain,
  Nor mark'st thy course with Death's delusive dye,
  But silent and unnoticed thou dost lie;
O'er life's soft springs thy venom dost diffuse,
  And, while thou givest new lustre to the eye,
While o'er the cheek are spread health's ruddy hues,
E'en then life's little rest thy cruel power subdues.

Oft I've beheld thee, in the glow of youth,
  Hid 'neath the blushing roses which there bloom'd;
And dropp'd a tear, for then thy cankering tooth
  I knew would never stay, till all consumed,
  In the cold vault of death he were entomb'd.

But oh! what sorrow did I feel, as swift,
  Insidious ravager, I saw thee fly
Through fair Lucina's breast of whitest snow,
  Preparing swift her passage to the sky.
Though still intelligence beam'd in the glance,
  The liquid lustre of her fine blue eye;
Yet soon did languid listlessness advance,
And soon she camly sunk in death's repugnant trance.

Even when her end was swiftly drawing near,
  And dissolution hover'd o'er her head:
Even then so beauteous did her form appear,
  That none who saw her but admiring said,
  Sure so much beauty never could be dead.
Yet the dark lash of her expressive eye
Bent lowly down upon the languid —

. . . . . . . . .

## FRAGMENT.

Loud rage the winds without. — The wintry cloud
O'er the cold northstar casts her flitting shroud;
And Silence, pausing in some snow-clad dale,
Starts as she hears, by fits, the shrieking gale;
Where now, shut out from every still retreat,
Her pine-clad summit, and her woodland seat,
Shall Meditation, in her saddest mood,
Retire o'er all her pensive stores to brood?
Shivering and blue the peasant eyes askance
The drifted fleeces that around him dance,
And hurries on his half-averted form,
Stemming the fury of the sidelong storm.
Him soon shall greet his snow-topp'd [cot of thatch],
Soon shall his numb'd hand tremble on the latch,
Soon from his chimney's nook the cheerful flame
Diffuse a genial warmth throughout his frame;
Round the light fire, while roars the north wind loud,
What merry groups of vacant faces crowd;

These hail his coming — these his meal prepare,
And boast in all that cot no lurking care.
 What though the social circle be denied,
Even Sadness brightens at her own fireside,
Loves, with fix'd eye, to watch the fluttering blaze,
While musing Memory dwells on former days;
Or Hope, bless'd spirit! smiles — and still forgiven,
Forgets the passport, while she points to Heaven.
Then heap the fire — shut out the biting air,
And from its station wheel the easy chair:
Thus fenced and warm, in silent fit, 'tis sweet
To hear without the bitter tempest beat,
All, all alone — to sit, and muse, and sigh,
The pensive tenant of obscurity.

. . . . . . . . .

## TO A FRIEND IN DISTRESS,

WHO, WHEN THE AUTHOR REASONED WITH HIM CALMLY, ASKED, "IF HE DID NOT FEEL FOR HIM."

"Do I not feel?" The doubt is keen as steel.
Yea, I do feel — most exquisitely feel;
My heart can weep, when, from my downcast eye,
I chase the tear, and stem the rising sigh:
Deep buried there I close the rankling dart,
And smile the most when heaviest is my heart.
On this I act — whatever pangs surround,
'Tis magnanimity to hide the wound!

When all was new, and life was in its spring,
I lived an unloved, solitary thing;
Even then I learn'd to bury deep from day
The piercing cares that wore my youth away:
Even then I learn'd for others' cares to feel;
Even then I wept I had not power to heal:
Even then, deep-sounding through the nightly gloom,
I heard the wretched's groan, and mourn'd the wretched's doom.
Who were my friends in youth? — The midnight fire —
The silent moonbeam, or the starry choir;
To these I 'plain'd, or turn'd from outer sight,
To bless my lonely taper's friendly light;
I never yet could ask, howe'er forlorn,
For vulgar pity mix'd with vulgar scorn;
The sacred source of woe I never ope,
My breast 's my coffer, and my God 's my hope.
But that I do feel, Time, my friend, will show,
Though the cold crowd the secret never know;
With them I laugh — yet, when no eye can see,
I weep for nature, and I weep for thee.
Yes, thou didst wrong me, . . .; I fondly thought,
In thee I 'd found the friend my heart had sought!
I fondly thought, that thou couldst pierce the guise,
And read the truth that in my bosom lies;
I fondly thought, ere Time's last days were gone,
Thy heart and mine had mingled into one!
Yes — and they yet will mingle. Days and years
Will fly, and leave us partners in our tears:

We then shall feel that friendship has a power
To soothe affliction in her darkest hour;
Time's trial o'er, shall clasp each other's hand,
And wait the passport to a better land.

Thine,

H. K. WHITE.

Half past Eleven o'clock at Night.

## CHRISTMAS DAY.

1804.

YET once more, and once more, awake, my Harp,
From silence and neglect — one lofty strain;
Lofty, yet wilder than the winds of Heaven,
And speaking mysteries more than words can tell,
I ask of thee; for I, with hymnings high,
Would join the dirge of the departing year.
Yet with no wintry garland from the woods,
Wrought of the leafless branch, or ivy sear,
Wreathe I thy tresses, dark December! now;
Me higher quarrel calls, with loudest song,
And fearful joy, to celebrate the day
Of the Redeemer. — Near two thousand suns
Have set their seals upon the rolling lapse
Of generations, since the dayspring first
Beam'd from on high! — Now to the mighty mass
Of that increasing aggregate we add
One unit more. Space in comparison
How small, yet mark'd with how much misery;

Wars, famines, and the fury, Pestilence,
Over the nations hanging her dread scourge;
The oppressed, too, in silent bitterness,
Weeping their sufferance; and the arm of wrong,
Forcing the scanty portion from the weak,
And steeping the lone widow's couch with tears.
So has the year been character'd with woe
In Christian land, and mark'd with wrongs and crimes;
Yet 't was not thus He taught—not thus He lived,
Whose birth we this day celebrate with prayer
And much thanksgiving. He, a man of woes,
Went on the way appointed,—path, though rude,
Yet borne with patience still:—He came to cheer
The broken-hearted, to raise up the sick,
And on the wandering and benighted mind
To pour the light of truth. O task divine!
O more than angel teacher! He had words
To soothe the barking waves, and hush the winds;
And when the soul was toss'd in troubled seas,
Wrapp'd in thick darkness and the howling storm,
He, pointing to the star of peace on high,
Arm'd it with holy fortitude, and bade it smile
At the surrounding wreck.——
When with deep agony his heart was rack'd,
Not for himself the tear-drop dew'd his cheek,
For them He wept, for them to Heaven He pray'd,
His persecutors—"Father, pardon them,
They know not what they do."
Angels of Heaven,
Ye who beheld Him fainting on the cross,

And did him homage, say, may mortal join
The halleluiahs of the risen God?
Will the faint voice and grovelling song be heard
Amid the seraphim in light divine?
Yes, he will deign, the Prince of Peace will deign,
For mercy, to accept the hymn of faith,
Low though it be and humble. Lord of life,
The Christ, the Comforter, thine advent now
Fills my uprising soul.—I mount, I fly
Far o'er the skies, beyond the rolling orbs;
The bonds of flesh dissolve, and earth recedes,
And care, and pain, and sorrow are no more.

. . . . . . . . . .

## NELSONI MORS.

Yet once again, my Harp, yet once again
One ditty more, and on the mountain ash
I will again suspend thee. I have felt
The warm tear frequent on my cheek, since last,
At eventide, when all the winds were hush'd,
I woke to thee the melancholy song.
Since then with Thoughtfulness, a maid severe,
I've journey'd, and have learn'd to shape the freaks
Of frolic fancy to the line of truth;
Not unrepining, for my froward heart
Stills turns to thee, mine Harp, and to the flow
Of spring-gales past—the woods and storied haunts
Of my not songless boyhood.—Yet once more,
Not fearless, I will wake thy tremulous tones,

My long-neglected Harp. He must not sink;
The good, the brave — he must not, shall not sink
Without the meed of some melodious tear.
  Though from the Muse's chalice I may pour
No precious dews of Aganippe's well,
Or Castaly, — though from the morning cloud
I fetch no hues to scatter on his hearse:
Yet will I wreathe a garland for his brows,
Of simple flowers, such as the hedge-rows scent
Of Britain, my loved country; and with tears
Most eloquent, yet silent, I will bathe
Thy honour'd corse, my Nelson, tears as warm
And honest as the ebbing blood that flow'd
Fast from thy honest heart. Thou, Pity, too,
If ever I have loved, with faltering step,
To follow thee in the cold and starless night,
To the top-crag of some rain-beaten cliff;
And, as I heard the deep gun bursting loud
Amid the pauses of the storm, have pour'd
Wild strains, and mournful, to the hurrying winds,
The dying soul's viaticum; if oft
Amid the carnage of the field I've sate
With thee upon the moonlight throne, and sung
To cheer the fainting soldier's dying soul,
With mercy and forgiveness — visitant
Of Heaven — sit thou upon my harp,
And give it feeling, which were else too cold
For argument so great, for theme so high.
  How dimly on that morn the sun arose,
'Kerchief'd in mists, and tearful, when —

. . . . . . . . . . .

## EPIGRAM ON ROBERT BLOOMFIELD.

Bloomfield, thy happy omen'd name
Ensures continuance to thy fame;
Both sense and truth this verdict give,
While fields shall bloom, thy name shall live!

---

## ELEGY

OCCASIONED BY THE DEATH OF MR. GILL, WHO WAS DROWNED IN THE RIVER TRENT, WHILE BATHING, 9TH AUGUST, 1802.

He sunk, the impetuous river roll'd along,
  The sullen wave betray'd his dying breath;
And rising sad the rustling sedge among,
  The gale of evening touch'd the cords of death.

Nymph of the Trent! why didst thou not appear
  To snatch the victim from thy felon wave!
Alas! too late thou camest to embalm his bier,
  And deck with waterflags his early grave.

Triumphant, riding o'er its tumid prey,
  Rolls the red stream in sanguinary pride;
While anxious crowds, in vain, expectant stay,
  And ask the swoln corse from the murdering tide.

The stealing tear-drop stagnates in the eye,
  The sudden sigh by friendship's bosom proved,
I mark them rise — I mark the general sigh!
  Unhappy youth! and wert thou so beloved?

On thee, as lone I trace the Trent's green brink,
  When the dim twilight slumbers on the glade;
On thee my thoughts shall dwell, nor Fancy shrink
  To hold mysterious converse with thy shade.

Of thee, as early, I, with vagrant feet,
  Hail the gray-sandal'd morn in Colwick's vale,
Of thee my sylvan reed shall warble sweet,
  And wild-wood echoes shall repeat the tale.

And, oh! ye nymphs of Pæon! who preside
  O'er running rill and salutary stream.
Guard ye in future well the halcyon tide
  From the rude death-shriek and the dying scream.

---

## INSCRIPTION FOR A MONUMENT TO THE MEMORY OF COWPER.

  Reader! if with no vulgar sympathy
Thou view'st the wreck of genius and of worth,
Stay thou thy footsteps near this hallow'd spot.
Here Cowper rests. Although renown have made
His name familiar to thine ear, this stone
May tell thee that his virtues were above
The common portion: — that the voice, now hush'd

In death, was once serenely querulous
With pity's tones, and in the ear of woe
Spake music. Now, forgetful, at thy feet,
His tired head presses on its last long rest,
Still tenant of the tomb; — and on the cheek,
Once warm with animation's lambent flush,
Sits the pale image of unmark'd decay.
Yet mourn not. He had chosen the better part;
And, these sad garments of Mortality
Put off, we trust, that to a happier land
He went a light and gladsome passenger.
Sigh'st thou for honours, reader? Call to mind
That glory's voice is impotent to pierce
The silence of the tomb! but virtue blooms
Even on the wreck of life, and mounts the skies.
So gird thy loins with lowliness, and walk
With Cowper on the pilgrimage of Christ.

---

## "I'M PLEASED, AND YET I'M SAD.

When twilight steals along the ground,
And all the bells are ringing round,
    One, two, three, four, and five,
I at my study window sit,
And, wrapp'd in many a musing fit,
    To bliss am all alive.

But though impressions calm and sweet
Thrill round my heart a holy heat,
    And I am inly glad;

The tear-drop stands in either eye,
And yet I cannot tell thee why,
I'm pleased, and yet I'm sad.

The silvery rack that flies away,
Like mortal life or pleasure's ray,
Does that disturb my breast?
Nay, what have I, a studious man,
To do with life's unstable plan,
Or pleasure's fading vest?

Is it that here I must not stop,
But o'er yon blue hill's woody top
Must bend my lonely way?
No, surely no! for give but me
My own fireside, and I shall be
At home where'er I stray.

Then is it that yon steeple there,
With music sweet shall fill the air,
When thou no more canst hear?
Oh, no! oh, no! for then, forgiven,
I shall be with my God in heaven,
Released from every fear.

Then whence it is I cannot tell,
But there is some mysterious spell
That holds me when I'm glad;
And so the tear-drop fills my eye,
When yet in truth I know not why,
Or wherefore I am sad.

## SOLITUDE.

It is not that my lot is low,
That bids this silent tear to flow;
It is not grief that bids me moan;
It is that I am all alone.

In woods and glens I love to roam,
When the tired hedger hies him home;
Or by the woodland pool to rest,
When pale the star looks on its breast.

Yet when the silent evening sighs,
With hallow'd airs and symphonies,
My spirit takes another tone,
And sighs that it is all alone.

The autumn leaf is sere and dead,
It floats upon the water's bed;
I would not be a leaf, to die
Without recording sorrow's sigh!

The woods and winds, with sullen wail,
Tell all the same unvaried tale;
I've none to smile when I am free,
And when I sigh, to sigh with me.

Yet in my dreams a form I view,
That thinks on me, and loves me too;
I start, and when the vision's flown,
I weep that I am all alone.

If far from me the Fates remove
Domestic peace, connubial love,
The prattling ring, the social cheer,
Affection's voice, affection's tear,
Ye sterner powers, that bind the heart,
To me your iron aid impart!
O teach me when the nights are chill,
And my fireside is lone and still;
When to the blaze that crackles near,
I turn a tired and pensive ear,
And Nature conquering bids me sigh
For love's soft accents whispering nigh;
O teach me, on that heavenly road,
That leads to Truth's occult abode,
To wrap my soul in dreams sublime,
Till earth and care no more be mine.
Let bless'd Philosophy impart
Her soothing measures to my heart;
And while with Plato's ravish'd ears
I list the music of the spheres,
Or on the mystic symbols pore,
That hide the Chald's sublimer lore,
I shall not brood on summers gone,
Nor think that I am all alone.

Fanny! upon thy breast I may not lie!
  Fanny! thou dost not hear me when I speak!
Where art thou, love?—Around I turn my eye,
  And as I turn, the tear is on my cheek.

Was it a dream? or did my love behold
 Indeed my lonely couch?—Methought the breath
Fann'd not her bloodless lip; her eye was cold
 And hollow, and the livery of death
Invested her pale forehead. Sainted maid!
 My thoughts oft rest with thee in thy cold grave,
 Through the long wintry night, when wind and wave
Rock the dark house where thy poor head is laid.
Yet, hush! my fond heart, hush! there is a shore
 Of better promise; and I know at last,
 When the long sabbath of the tomb is past,
We two shall meet in Christ—to part no more.

## FRAGMENTS.*

SAW'ST thou that light? exclaim'd the youth, and paused:
Through yon dark firs it glanced, and on the stream
That skirts the woods it for a moment play'd.
Again, more light it gleam'd,—or does some sprite
Delude mine eyes with shapes of wood and streams,
And lamp far beaming through the thicket's gloom,
As from some bosom'd cabin, where the voice
Of revelry, or thrifty watchfulness,
Keeps in the lights at this unwonted hour?
No sprite deludes mine eyes,—the beam now glows

* These Fragments were written upon the back of his mathematical papers, during the last year of his life.

With steady lustre. — Can it be the moon
Who, hidden long by the invidious veil
That blots the Heavens, now sets behind the woods?
No moon to-night has look'd upon the sea
Of clouds beneath her, answer'd Rudiger,
She has been sleeping with Endymion.

. . . . . . .

THE pious man,
In this bad world, when mists and couchant storms
Hide Heaven's fine circlet, springs aloft in faith
Above the clouds that threat him, to the fields
Of ether, where the day is never veil'd
With intervening vapours, and looks down
Serene upon the troublous sea, that hides
The earth's fair breast, that sea whose nether face
To grovelling mortals frowns and darkens all;
But on whose billowy back, from man conceal'd,
The glaring sunbeam plays.

Lo! on the eastern summit, clad in gray,
Morn, like a horseman girt for travel, comes,
And from his tower of mist,
Night's watchman hurries down.

THERE was a little bird upon that pile;
It perch'd upon a ruin'd pinnacle,
And made sweet melody.

The song was soft, yet cheerful, and most clear,
For other note none swell'd the air but his.
It seem'd as if the little chorister,
Sole tenant of the melancholy pile,
Were a lone hermit, outcast from his kind,
Yet withal cheerful. I have heard the note
Echoing so lonely o'er the aisle forlorn,
—— Much musing ——

O PALE art thou, my lamp, and faint
Thy melancholy ray:
When the still night's unclouded saint
Is walking on her way.
Through my lattice leaf embower'd,
Fair she sheds her shadowy beam,
And o'er my silent sacred room
Casts a checker'd twilight gloom;
I throw aside the learned sheet,
I cannot choose but gaze, she looks so mildly sweet.
Sad vestal, why art thou so fair,
Or why am I so frail?

Methinks thou lookest kindly on me, Moon,
And cheerest my lone hours with sweet regards!
Surely like me thou 'rt sad, but dost not speak
Thy sadness to the cold unheeding crowd;
So mournfully composed, o'er yonder cloud
Thou shinest, like a cresset, beaming far
From the rude watch-tower, o'er the Atlantic wave.

O GIVE me music — for my soul doth faint;
  I'm sick of noise and care, and now mine ear
Longs for some air of peace, some dying plaint,
  That may the spirit from its cell unsphere.

Hark how it falls! and now it steals along,
  Like distant bells upon the lake at eve,
When all is still; and now it grows more strong,
  As when the choral train their dirges weave,
Mellow and many-voiced; where every close,
  O'er the old minster roof, in echoing waves re-
    flows.

Oh! I am wrapt aloft. My spirit soars
  Beyond the skies, and leaves the stars behind.
Lo! angels lead me to the happy shores,
  And floating pæans fill the buoyant wind.
Farewell! base earth, farewell! my soul is freed,
Far from its clayey cell it springs, —

. . . . . .

AND must thou go, and must we part?
    Yes, Fate decrees, and I submit;
The pang that rends in twain my heart,
    Oh, Fanny, dost thou share in it?

Thy sex is fickle, — when away,
    Some happier youth may win thy ——

. . . . . .

Ah! who can say, however fair his view,
Through what sad scenes his path may lie?
Ah! who can give to others' woes his sigh,
Secure his own will never need it too?

Let thoughtless youth its seeming joys pursue,
Soon will they learn to scan with thoughtful eye
The illusive past and dark futurity;
Soon will they know—

. . . . . .

Hush'd is the lyre—the hand that swept
The low and pensive wires,
Robb'd of its cunning, from the task retires.

Yes—it is still—the lyre is still;
The spirit which its slumbers broke
Hath pass'd away,—and that weak hand that woke
Its forest melodies hath lost its skill.

Yet I would press you to my lips once more,
Ye wild, yet withering flowers of poesy;
Yet would I drink the fragrance which ye pour,
Mix'd with decaying odours: for to me
Ye have beguiled the hours of infancy,
As in the wood-paths of my native—

. . . . . .

When high romance o'er every wood and stream
  Dark lustre shed, my infant mind to fire,
Spell-struck, and fill'd with many a wondering dream,
  First in the groves I woke the pensive lyre.
All there was mystery then, the gust that woke
  The midnight echo was a spirit's dirge,
And unseen fairies would the moon invoke
  To their light morrice by the restless surge.
Now to my sober'd thought with life's false smiles,
  Too much . . .
The vagrant Fancy spreads no more her wiles,
  And dark forebodings now my bosom fill.

Once more, and yet once more,
    I give unto my harp a dark woven lay;
I heard the waters roar,
    I heard the flood of ages pass away.
O thou, stern spirit, who dost dwell
    In thine eternal cell,
Noting, gray chronicler! the silent years,
    I saw thee rise,—I saw the scroll complete,
    Thou spakest, and at thy feet
      The universe gave way.

## FRAGMENT OF AN ECCENTRIC DRAMA.

### WRITTEN AT A VERY EARLY AGE.

### THE DANCE OF THE CONSUMPTIVES.

Ding-dong! ding-dong!
Merry, merry go the bells,
Ding-dong! ding-dong!
Over the heath, over the moor, and over the dale,
"Swinging slow with sullen roar,"
Dance, dance away the jocund roundelay!
Ding-dong, ding-dong calls us away.

Round the oak, and round the elm,
Merrily foot it o'er the ground!
The sentry ghost it stands aloof,
So merrily, merrily foot it round.
Ding-dong! ding-dong!
Merry, merry go the bells,
Swelling in the nightly gale,
The sentry ghost,
It keeps its post,
And soon, and soon our sports must fail:
But let us trip the nightly ground,
While the merry, merry bells ring round.

Hark! Hark! the deathwatch ticks!
See, see, the winding-sheet!
Our dance is done,
Our race is run,
And we must lie at the alder's feet!
Ding-dong! ding-dong!
Merry, merry go the bells,
Swinging o'er the weltering wave!
And we must seek
Our deathbeds bleak,
Where the green sod grows upon the grave.

They vanish — The Goddess of Consumption descends, habited in a sky-blue robe, attended by mournful music.

Come, Melancholy, sister mine!
Cold the dews, and chill the night!
Come from thy dreary shrine!
The wan moon climbs the heavenly height,
And underneath her sickly ray
Troops of squalid spectres play,
And the dying mortals' groan
Startles the night on her dusky throne.
Come, come, sister mine!
Gliding on the pale moonshine:
We 'll ride at ease
On the tainted breeze,
And oh! our sport will be divine.

The Goddess of Melancholy advances out of a deep glen in the rear, habited in black, and covered with a thick veil. — She speaks.

Sister, from my dark abode,
Where nests the raven, sits the toad,
Hither I come, at thy command:
Sister, sister, join thy hand!
I will smooth the way for thee,
Thou shalt furnish food for me.
Come, let us speed our way
Where the troops of spectres play.
To charnel-houses, churchyards drear,
Where Death sits with a horrible leer,
A lasting grin, on a throne of bones,
And skim along the blue tombstones.
Come, let us speed away,
Lay our snares, and spread our tether!
I will smooth the way for thee,
Thou shalt furnish food for me;
And the grass shall wave
O'er many a grave,
Where youth and beauty sleep together.

### CONSUMPTION.

Come, let us speed our way,
Join our hands, and spread our tether!
I will furnish food for thee,
Thou shalt smooth the way for me!
And the grass shall wave
O'er many a grave,
Where youth and beauty sleep together.

### MELANCHOLY.

Hist, sister, hist! who comes here?
Oh! I know her by that tear,
By that blue eye's languid glare,
By her skin, and by her hair:
She is mine,
And she is thine,
Now the deadliest draught prepare.

### CONSUMPTION.

In the dismal night air dress'd,
I will creep into her breast:
Flush her cheek, and bleach her skin,
And feed on the vital fire within.
Lover, do not trust her eyes, —
When they sparkle most, she dies!
Mother, do not trust her breath, —
Comfort she will breathe in death!
Father, do not strive to save her, —
She is mine, and I must have her!
The coffin must be her bridal bed!
The winding-sheet must wrap her head;
The whispering winds must o'er her sigh,
For soon in the grave the maid must lie:
The worm it will riot
On heavenly diet,
When death has deflower'd her eye.

[They vanish.
While Consumption speaks, Angelina enters.

## ANGELINA.

With * what a silent and dejected pace
Dost thou, wan Moon! upon thy way advance
In the blue welkin's vault! — Pale wanderer!
Hast thou too felt the pangs of hopeless love,
That thus, with such a melancholy grace,
Thou dost pursue thy solitary course?
Has thy Endymion, smooth-faced boy, forsook
Thy widow'd breast — on which the spoiler oft
Has nestled fondly, while the silver clouds
Fantastic pillow'd thee, and the dim night,
Obsequious to thy will, encurtain'd round
With its thick fringe thy couch? Wan traveller,
How like thy fate to mine! — Yet I have still
One heavenly hope remaining, which thou lack'st;
My woes will soon be buried in the grave
Of kind forgetfulness — my journey here,
Though it be darksome, joyless, and forlorn,
Is yet but short, and soon my weary feet
Will greet the peaceful inn of lasting rest.
But thou, unhappy Queen! art doom'd to trace
Thy lonely walk in the drear realms of night,
While many a lagging age shall sweep beneath
The leaden pinions of unshaken time;
Though not a hope shall spread its glittering hue
To cheat thy steps along the weary way.

* With how sad steps, O Moon! thou climb'st the skies,
How silently, and with how wan a face!
*Sir P. Sidney.*

O that the sum of human happiness
Should be so trifling, and so frail withal,
That when possess'd, it is but lessen'd grief;
And even then there 's scarce a sudden gust
That blows across the dismal waste of life,
But bears it from the view. Oh! who would shun
The hour that cuts from earth, and fear to press
The calm and peaceful pillows of the grave,
And yet endure the various ills of life,
And dark vicissitudes! Soon, I hope, I feel,
And am assured, that I shall lay my dead,
My weary aching head, on its last rest,
And on my lowly bed the grass-green sod
Will flourish sweetly. And then they will weep
That one so young, and what they 're pleased to call
So beautiful, should die so soon. And tell
How painful Disappointment's canker'd fang
Wither'd the rose upon my maiden cheek.
Oh, foolish ones! why, I shall sleep so sweetly,
Laid in my darksome grave, that they themselves
Might envy me my rest! And as for them,
Who, on the score of former intimacy,
May thus remembrance me — they must themselves
Successive fall.
Around the winter fire
(When out-a-doors the biting frost congeals,
And shrill the skater's irons on the pool
Ring loud, as by the moonlight he performs
His graceful evolutions) they not long
Shall sit and chat of older times, and feats

Of early youth, but silent, one by one,
Shall drop into their shrouds. Some, in their age,
Ripe for the sickle; others young, like me,
And falling green beneath the untimely stroke.
Thus, in short time, in the churchyard forlorn,
Where I shall lie, my friends will lay them down,
And dwell with me, a happy family.
And oh! thou cruel, yet beloved youth,
Who now hast left me hopeless here to mourn,
Do thou but shed one tear upon my corse
And say that I was gentle, and deserved
A better lover, and I shall forgive
All, all thy wrongs; — and then do thou forget
The hapless Margaret, and be as bless'd
As wish can make thee — Laugh, and play, and sing
With thy dear choice, and never think of me.
    Yet hist, I hear a step. — In this dark wood —

. . . . . . . . .

## TO A FRIEND.

### WRITTEN AT A VERY EARLY AGE.

I've read, my friend, of Dioclesian,
And many another noble Grecian,
Who wealth and palaces resign'd,
In cots the joys of peace to find;
Maximian's meal of turnip-tops
(Disgusting food to dainty chops)

I 've also read of, without wonder;
But such a cursed egregious blunder,
As that a man of wit and sense
Should leave his books to hoard up pence, —
Forsake the loved Aonian maids
For all the petty tricks of trades,
I never, either now, or long since,
Have heard of such a peace of nonsense;
That one who learning's joys hath felt,
And at the Muse's altar knelt,
Should leave a life of sacred leisure
To taste the accumulating pleasure;
And, metamorphosed to an alley duck,
Grovel in loads of kindred muck.
Oh! 't is beyond my comprehension!
A courtier throwing up his pension, —
A lawyer working without a fee, —
A parson giving charity, —
A truly pious methodist preacher, —
Are not, egad, so out of nature.
Had nature made thee half a fool,
But given thee wit to keep a school,
I had not stared at thy backsliding:
But when thy wit I can confide in,
When well I know thy just pretence
To solid and exalted sense;
When well I know that on thy head
Philosophy her lights hath shed,
I stand aghast! thy virtues sum to,
I wonder what this world will come to!

Yet, whence this strain? shall I repine
That thou alone dost singly shine?
Shall I lament that thou alone,
Of men of parts, hast prudence known?

---

## LINES

### ON READING THE POEMS OF WARTON. AGE FOURTEEN.

Oh, Warton! to thy soothing shell,
Stretch'd remote in hermit cell,
Where the brook runs babbling by,
For ever I could listening lie;
And catching all the muses' fire,
Hold converse with the tuneful quire.

What pleasing themes thy page adorn,
The ruddy streaks of cheerful morn,
The pastoral pipe, the ode sublime,
And Melancholy's mournful chime!
Each with unwonted graces shines
In thy ever lovely lines.

Thy muse deserves the lasting meed;
Attuning sweet the Dorian reed,
Now the lovelorn swain complains,
And sings his sorrows to the plains;
Now the sylvan scenes appear
Through all the changes of the year;

Or the elegiac strain
Softly sings of mental pain,
And mournful diapasons sail
On the faintly dying gale.
    But, ah! the soothing scene is o'er,
    On middle flight we cease to soar,
For now the muse assumes a bolder sweep,
Strikes on the lyric string her sorrows deep,
    In strains unheard before.
Now, now the rising fire thrills high,
Now, now to heaven's high realms we fly,
    And every throne explore:
The soul entranced, on mighty wings,
With all the poet's heat upsprings,
    And loses earthly woes;
Till all alarm'd at the giddy height,
The Muse descends on gentler flight,
    And lulls the wearied soul to soft repose.

## FRAGMENT.

The western gale,
Mild as the kisses of connubial love,
Plays round my languid limbs, as all dissolved,
Beneath the ancient elm's fantastic shade
I lie, exhausted with the noontide heat:
While rippling o'er its deep worn pebble bed,
The rapid rivulet rushes at my feet,
Dispensing coolness. On the fringed marge

Full many a floweret rears its head, — or pink,
Or gaudy daffodil. 'Tis here, at noon,
The buskin'd wood-nymphs from the heat retire,
And lave them in the fountain; here secure
From Pan, or savage satyr, they disport:
Or stretch'd supinely on the velvet turf,
Lull'd by the laden bee, or sultry fly,
Invoke the god of slumber. . . .
. . . . . . . .

And, hark! how merrily, from distant tower,
Ring round the village bells! now on the gale
They rise with gradual swell, distinct and loud;
Anon they die upon the pensive ear,
Melting in faintest music. They bespeak
A day of jubilee, and oft they bear,
Commix'd along the unfrequented shore,
The sound of village dance and tabor loud,
Startling the musing ear of Solitude.
Such is the jocund wake of Whitsuntide,
When happy Superstition, gabbling eld!
Holds her unhurtful gambols. All the day
The rustic revellers ply the mazy dance
On the smooth shaven green, and then at eve
Commence the harmless rites and auguries;
And many a tale of ancient days goes round.
They tell of wizard seer, whose potent spells
Could hold in dreadful thrall the labouring moon,
Or draw the fix'd stars from their eminence,
And still the midnight tempest. Then anon
Tell of uncharnel'd spectres, seen to glide

Along the lone wood's unfrequented path,
Startling the 'nighted traveller; while the sound
Of undistinguish'd murmurs, heard to come
From the dark centre of the deepening glen,
Struck on his frozen ear.
Oh, Ignorance!
Thou art fallen man's best friend! With thee he [speeds
In frigid apathy along his way.
And never does the tear of agony
Burn down his scorching cheek; or the keen steel
Of wounded feeling penetrate his breast.
E'en now, as leaning on this fragrant bank,
I taste of all the keener happiness
Which sense refined affords — E'en now my heart
Would fain induce me to forsake the world,
Throw off these garments, and in shepherd's weeds,
With a small flock, and short suspended reed,
To sojourn in the woodland. — Then my thought
Draws such gay pictures of ideal bliss,
That I could almost err in reason's spite,
And trespass on my judgment.
Such is life:
The distant prospect always seems more fair,
And when attain'd, another still succeeds,
Far fairer than before, — yet compass'd round
With the same dangers, and the same dismay.
And we poor pilgrims in this dreary maze,
Still discontented, chase the fairy form
Of unsubstantial Happiness, to find,
When life itself is sinking in the strife,
'Tis but an airy bubble and a cheat.

## COMMENCEMENT OF A POEM ON DESPAIR.

Some to Aonian lyres of silver sound
With winning elegance attune their song,
Form'd to sink lightly on the soothed sense,
And charm the soul with softest harmony:
'Tis then that Hope with sanguine eye is seen
Roving through Fancy's gay futurity;
Her heart light dancing to the sounds of pleasure,
Pleasure of days to come. Memory, too, then
Comes with her sister, Melancholy sad,
Pensively musing on the scenes of youth,
Scenes never to return.*
Such subjects merit poets used to raise
The attic verse harmonious; but for me
A deadlier theme demands my backward hand,
And bids me strike the strings of dissonance
With frantic energy.
'Tis wan Despair I sing, if sing I can
Of him before whose blast the voice of Song,
And Mirth, and Hope, and Happiness all fly,
Nor ever dare return. His notes are heard
At noon of night, where, on the coast of blood,
The lacerated son of Angola
Howls forth his sufferings to the moaning wind;
And, when the awful silence of the night
Strikes the chill death-dew to the murderer's heart,
He speaks in every conscience-prompted word

* Alluding to the two pleasing poems, the Pleasures of Hope and of Memory.

Half utter'd, half suppress'd.
'Tis him I sing — Despair — terrific name,
Striking unsteadily the tremulous chord
Of timorous terror — discord in the sound:
For to a theme revolting as is this,
Dare not I woo the maids of harmony,
Who love to sit and catch the soothing sound
Of lyre Æolian, or the martial bugle,
Calling the hero to the field of glory,
And firing him with deeds of high emprise
And warlike triumph: but from scenes like mine
Shrink they affrighted, and detest the bard
Who dares to sound the hollow tones of horror.
Hence, then, soft maids,
And woo the silken zephyr in the bowers
By Heliconia's sleep-inviting stream:
For aid like yours I seek not; 'tis for powers
Of darker hue to inspire a verse like mine!
'Tis work for wizards, sorcerers, and fiends.
Hither, ye furious imps of Acheron,
Nurslings of hell, and beings shunning light,
And all the myriads of the burning concave:
Souls of the damned: — Hither, oh! come and join
The infernal chorus. 'Tis Despair I sing!
He, whose sole tooth inflicts a deadlier pang
Than all your tortures join'd. Sing, sing Despair!
Repeat the sound, and celebrate his power;
Unite shouts, screams, and agonizing shrieks,
Till the loud pæan ring through hell's high vault,
And the remotest spirits of the deep
Leap from the lake, and join the dreadful song.

## THE EVE OF DEATH.

IRREGULAR.

Silence of death — portentous calm,
Those airy forms that yonder fly
Denote that your void foreruns a storm,
That the hour of fate is nigh.
I see, I see, on the dim mist borne,
The Spirit of battles rear his crest!
I see, I see, that ere the morn,
His spear will forsake its hated rest,
And the widow'd wife of Larrendill will beat her naked breast.

O'er the smooth bosom of the sullen deep,
No softly ruffling zephyrs fly;
But nature sleeps a deathless sleep,
For the hour of battle is nigh.
Not a loose leaf waves on the dusky oak,
But a creeping stillness reigns around;
Except when the raven, with ominous croak,
On the ear does unwelcomely sound.
I know, I know what this silence means;
I know what the raven saith —
Strike, oh, ye bards! the melancholy harp,
For this is the eve of death.

Behold, how along the twilight air
The shades of our fathers glide!

There Morven fled, with the blood-drench'd hair,
  And Colma with gray side.
No gale around its coolness flings,
  Yet sadly sigh the gloomy trees;
And hark! how the harp's unvisited strings
  Sound sweet, as if swept by a whispering breeze!
'Tis done! the sun he has set in blood!
  He will never set more to the brave;
Let us pour to the hero the dirge of death,
  For to-morrow he hies to the grave.

---

## THANATOS.

Oh! who would cherish life,
  And cling unto this heavy clog of clay,
  Love this rude world of strife,
Where glooms and tempests cloud the fairest day;
    And where, 'neath outward smiles,
  Conceal'd the snake lies feeding on its prey,
  Where pitfalls lie in every flowery way,
    And sirens lure the wanderer to their wiles!
  Hateful it is to me,
Its riotous railings and revengeful strife;
  I'm tired with all its screams and brutal shouts
Dinning the ear; — away — away with life!
    And welcome, oh! thou silent maid,
    Who in some foggy vault art laid,

Where never daylight's dazzling ray
Comes to disturb thy dismal sway;
And there amid unwholesome damps dost sleep,
In such forgetful slumbers deep,
That all thy senses stupefied
Are to marble petrified.
Sleepy Death, I welcome thee!
Sweet are thy calms to misery.
Poppies I will ask no more,
Nor the fatal hellebore;
Death is the best, the only cure,
His are slumbers ever sure.
Lay me in the Gothic tomb,
In whose solemn fretted gloom
I may lie in mouldering state,
With all the grandeur of the great:
Over me, magnificent,
Carve a stately monument;
Then thereon my statue lay,
With hands in attitude to pray,
And angels serve to hold my head,
Weeping o'er the father dead.
Duly too at close of day,
Let the pealing organ play;
And while the harmonious thunders roll,
Chant a vesper to my soul:
Thus how sweet my sleep will be,
Shut out from thoughtful misery!

## ATHANATOS.

Away with Death — away
With all her sluggish sleeps and chilling damps,
Impervious to the day,
Where nature sinks into inanity.
How can the soul desire
Such hateful nothingness to crave,
And yield with joy the vital fire
To moulder in the grave!
Yet mortal life is sad,
Eternal storms molest its sullen sky;
And sorrows ever rife
Drain the sacred fountain dry —
Away with mortal life!
But, hail the calm reality,
The seraph Immortality!
Hail the heavenly bowers of peace,
Where all the storms of passion cease.
Wild life's dismaying struggle o'er,
The wearied spirit weeps no more;
But wears the eternal smile of joy,
Tasting bliss without alloy.
Welcome, welcome, happy bowers,
Where no passing tempest lowers;
But the azure heavens display
The everlasting smile of day;

Where the choral seraph choir
Strike to praise the harmonious lyre;
And the spirit sinks to ease,
Lull'd by distant symphonies.
Oh! to think of meeting there
The friends whose graves received our tear,
The daughter loved, the wife adored,
To our widow'd arms restored;
And all the joys which death did sever,
Given to us again for ever!
Who would cling to wretched life,
And hug the poison'd thorn of strife;
Who would not long from earth to fly,
A sluggish senseless lump to lie,
When the glorious prospect lies
Full before his raptured eyes?

## MUSIC

WRITTEN BETWEEN THE AGES OF FOURTEEN AND FIFTEEN, WITH A FEW SUBSEQUENT VERBAL ALTERATIONS.

Music, all powerful o'er the human mind,
Can still each mental storm, each tumult calm,
Soothe anxious care on sleepless couch reclined,
And e'en fierce Anger's furious rage disarm.

At her command the various passions lie;
She stirs to battle, or she lulls to peace;

Melts the charm'd soul to thrilling ecstasy,
And bids the jarring world's harsh clangour cease.

Her martial sounds can fainting troops inspire
With strength unwonted, and enthusiasm raise;
Infuse new ardour, and with youthful fire
Urge on the warrior gray with length of days.

Far better she, when, with her soothing lyre,
She charms the falchion from the savage grasp,
And melting into pity vengeful ire,
Looses the bloody breastplate's iron clasp.

With her in pensive mood I long to roam,
At midnight's hour, or evening's calm decline,
And thoughtful o'er the falling streamlet's foam,
In calm seclusion's hermit walks recline.

Whilst mellow sounds from distant copse arise,
Of softest flute or reeds harmonic join'd,
With rapture thrill'd each worldly passion dies,
And pleased attention claims the passive mind.

Soft through the dell the dying strains retire,
Then burst majestic in the varied swell;
Now breathe melodious as the Grecian lyre,
Or on the ear in sinking cadence dwell.

Romantic sounds! such is the bliss ye give, [soul,
That heaven's bright scenes seem bursting on the
With joy I'd yield each sensual wish, to live
For ever 'neath your undefiled control.

Oh! surely melody from heaven was sent,
  To cheer the soul when tired with human strife,
To soothe the wayward heart by sorrow rent,
  And soften down the rugged road of life.

---

## ON BEING CONFINED TO SCHOOL ONE PLEASANT MORNING IN SPRING.

WRITTEN AT THE AGE OF THIRTEEN.

  The morning sun's enchanting rays
Now call forth every songster's praise;
Now the lark, with upward flight,
Gaily ushers in the light;
While wildly warbling from each tree,
The birds sing songs to Liberty.
  But for me no songster sings,
For me no joyous lark upsprings;
For I, confined in gloomy school,
Must own the pedant's iron rule,
And far from sylvan shades and bowers,
In durance vile must pass the hours;
There con the scholiast's dreary lines,
Where no bright ray of genius shines,
And close to rugged learning cling,
While laughs around the jocund spring.
How gladly would my soul forego
All that arithmeticians know,

Or stiff grammarians quaintly teach,
Or all that industry can reach,
To taste each morn of all the joys
That with the laughing sun arise;
And unconstrain'd to rove along
The bushy brakes and glens among;
And woo the muse's gentle power
In unfrequented rural bower:
But, ah! such heaven-approaching joys
Will never greet my longing eyes;
Still will they cheat in vision fine,
Yet never but in fancy shine.
  Oh, that I were the little wren
That shrilly chirps from yonder glen!
Oh, far away I then would rove
To some secluded bushy grove;
There hop and sing with careless glee,
Hop and sing at liberty;
And, till death should stop my lays,
Far from men would spend my days.

---

## TO CONTEMPLATION.

THEE do I own, the prompter of my joys,
The soother of my cares, inspiring peace;
And I will ne'er forsake thee. Men may rave,
And blame and censure me, that I don't tie
My every thought down to the desk, and spend

The morning of my life in adding figures
With accurate monotony: that so
The good things of the world may be my lot,
And I might taste the blessedness of wealth:
But, oh! I was not made for money getting;
For me no much respected plum awaits.
Nor civic honour, envied. For as still
I tried to cast with school dexterity
The interesting sums, my vagrant thoughts
Would quick revert to many a woodland haunt,
Which fond remembrance cherish'd, and the pen
Dropp'd from my senseless fingers as I pictured,
In my mind's eye, how on the shores of Trent
I erewhile wander'd with my early friends
In social intercourse. And then I'd think
How contrary pursuits had thrown us wide,
One from the other, scatter'd o'er the globe;
They were set down with sober steadiness,
Each to his occupation. I alone,
A wayward youth, misled by Fancy's vagaries,
Remain'd unsettled, insecure, and veering
With every wind to every point of the compass.
Yes, in the counting-house I could indulge
In fits of close abstraction; yea, amid
The busy bustling crowds could meditate,
And send my thoughts ten thousand leagues away
Beyond the Atlantic, resting on my friend.
Ay, Contemplation, even in earliest youth
I woo'd thy heavenly influence! I would walk
A weary way when all my toils were done,

To lay myself at night in some lone wood,
And hear the sweet song of the nightingale.
Oh, those were times of happiness, and still
To memory doubly dear; for growing years
Had not then taught me man was made to mourn;
And a short hour of solitary pleasure,
Stolen from sleep, was ample recompense
For all the hateful bustles of the day.
My opening mind was ductile then, and plastic,
And soon the marks of care were worn away,
While I was sway'd by every novel impulse,
Yielding to all the fancies of the hour.
But it has now assumed its character;
Mark'd by strong lineaments, its haughty tone,
Like the firm oak, would sooner break than bend.
Yet still, O Contemplation! I do love
To indulge thy solemn musings; still the same
With thee alone I know to melt and weep,
In thee alone delighting. Why along
The dusky tract of commerce should I toil,
When, with an easy competence content,
I can alone be happy; where with thee
I may enjoy the loveliness of Nature,
And loose the wings of Fancy? Thus alone
Can I partake of happiness on earth;
And to be happy here is man's chief end,
For to be happy he must needs be good.

## MY OWN CHARACTER.

### ADDRESSED (DURING ILLNESS) TO A LADY.

Dear Fanny, I mean, now I'm laid on the shelf,
To give you a sketch — ay, a sketch of myself.
'Tis a pitiful subject, I frankly confess,
And one it would puzzle a painter to dress;
But, however, here goes, and as sure as a gun,
I'll tell all my faults like a penitent nun;
For I know, for my Fanny, before I address her,
She wont be a cynical father confessor.
Come, come, 'twill not do! put that curling brow down;
You can't, for the soul of you, learn how to frown.
Well, first I premise, it's my honest conviction,
That my breast is a chaos of all contradiction;
Religious — deistic — now loyal and warm;
Then a dagger-drawn democrat hot for reform:
This moment a fop, that, sententious as Titus;
Democritus now, and anon Heraclitus;
Now laughing and pleased, like a child with a rattle;
Then vex'd to the soul with impertinent tattle;
Now moody and sad, now unthinking and gay,
To all points of the compass I veer in a day.
I'm proud and disdainful to Fortune's gay child,
But to Poverty's offspring submissive and mild;

As rude as a boor, and as rough in dispute;
Then as for politeness — oh! dear — I'm a brute!
I show no respect where I never can feel it;
And as for contempt, take no pains to conceal it.
And so in the suite, by these laudable ends,
I've a great many foes, and a very few friends.
And yet, my dear Fanny, there are who can feel
That this proud heart of mine is not fashion'd of steel.
It can love (can it not?) — it can hate, I am sure;
And it's friendly enough, though in friends it be poor.
For itself though it bleed not, for others it bleeds;
If it have not ripe virtues, I'm sure it's the seeds;
And though far from faultless, or even so-so,
I think it may pass as our worldly things go.
Well, I've told you my frailties without any gloss;
Then as to my virtues, I'm quite at a loss!
I think I'm devout, and yet I can't say,
But in process of time I may get the wrong way.
I'm a general lover, if that's commendation,
And yet can't withstand you know whose fascination.
But I find that amidst all my tricks and devices,
In fishing for virtues, I'm pulling up vices;
So as for the good, why, if I possess it,
I am not yet learned enough to express it.
You yourself must examine the lovelier side,
And after your every art you have tried,
Whatever my faults, I may venture to say,
Hypocrisy never will come in your way.

I am upright, I hope; I'm downright, I'm clear!
And I think my worst foe must allow I'm sincere;
And if ever sincerity glow'd in my breast,
'T is now when I swear ———— . .

---

## LINES WRITTEN IN WILFORD CHURCHYARD.

### ON RECOVERY FROM SICKNESS.

Here would I wish to sleep. This is the spot
Which I have long mark'd out to lay my bones in.
Tired out and wearied with the riotous world,
Beneath this yew I would be sepulchred.
It is a lovely spot! The sultry sun,
From his meridian height, endeavours vainly
To pierce the shadowy foliage, while the zephyr
Comes wafting gently o'er the rippling Trent,
And plays about my wan cheek. 'T is a nook
Most pleasant. Such a one perchance did Gray
Frequent, as with a vagrant muse he wanton'd.
Come, I will sit me down and meditate,
For I am wearied with my summer's walk;
And here I may repose in silent ease;
And thus, perchance, when life's sad journey's o'er,
My harass'd soul, in this same spot, may find
The haven of its rest — beneath this sod
Perchance may sleep it sweetly, sound as death.
I would not have my corpse cemented down

With brick and stone, defrauding the poor earth-
Of its predestined dues; no, I would lie [worm
Beneath a little hillock, grass o'ergrown,
Swath'd down with osiers, just as sleep the cotters.
Yet may not undistinguish'd be my grave;
But there at eve may some congenial soul
Duly resort, and shed a pious tear,
The good man's benison — no more I ask.
And, oh! (if heavenly beings may look down
From where, with cherubim, inspired they sit,
Upon this little dim-discover'd spot,
The earth,) then will I cast a glance below
On him who thus my ashes shall embalm;
And I will weep too, and will bless the wanderer,
Wishing he may not long be doom'd to pine
In this low-thoughted world of darkling woe,
But that, ere long, he reach his kindred skies.
  Yet 't was a silly thought, as if the body,
Mouldering beneath the surface of the earth,
Could taste the sweets of summer scenery,
And feel the freshness of the balmy breeze!
Yet nature speaks within the human bosom,
And, spite of reason, bids it look beyond
His narrow verge of being, and provide
A decent residence for its clayey shell,
Endear'd to it by time. And who would lay
His body in the city burial-place,
To be thrown up again by some rude sexton,
And yield its narrow house another tenant,
Ere the moist flesh had mingled with the dust,

Ere the tenacious hair had left the scalp,
Exposed to insult lewd, and wantonness?
No, I will lay me in the village ground;
There are the dead respected. The poor hind,
Unletter'd as he is, would scorn to invade
The silent resting place of death. I 've seen
The labourer, returning from his toil,
Here stay his steps, and call his children round,
And slowly spell the rudely sculptured rhymes,
And, in his rustic manner, moralize.
I 've mark'd with what a silent awe he 'd spoken,
With head uncover'd, his respectful manner,
And all the honours which he paid the grave,
And thought on cities, where e'en cemeteries,
Bestrew'd with all the emblems of mortality,
Are not protected from the drunken insolence
Of wassailers profane, and wanton havoc.
Grant, Heaven, that here my pilgrimage may close!
Yet, if this be denied, where'er my bones
May lie — or in the city's crowded bounds,
Or scatter'd wide o'er the huge sweep of waters,
Or left a prey on some deserted shore
To the rapacious cormorant, — yet still,
(For why should sober reason cast away
A thought which soothes the soul?) yet still my spirit
Shall wing its way to these my native regions,
And hover o'er this spot. Oh, then I 'll think
Of times when I was seated 'neath this yew
In solemn rumination; and will smile
With joy that I have got my long'd release.

## VERSES.

THOU base repiner at another's joy,
Whose eye turns green at merit not thine own,
Oh, far away from generous Britons fly,
And find on meaner climes a fitter throne.
Away, away, it shall not be,
Thou shalt not dare defile our plains;
The truly generous heart disdains
Thy meaner, lowlier fires, while he
Joys at another's joy, and smiles at other's jollity.

Triumphant monster! though thy schemes succeed —
Schemes laid in Acheron, the brood of night,
Yet, but a little while, and nobly freed,
Thy happy victim will emerge to light;
When o'er his head in silence that reposes
Some kindred soul shall come to drop a tear;
Then will his last cold pillow turn to roses,
Which thou hadst planted with the thorn severe;
Then will thy baseness stand confess'd, and all
Will curse the ungenerous fate, that bade a Poet fall.

. . . . . . . .

Yet, ah! thy arrows are too keen, too sure:
  Couldst thou not pitch upon another prey?
Alas! in robbing him thou robb'st the poor,
  Who only boast what thou wouldst take away.
See the lone Bard at midnight study sitting,
  O'er his pale features streams his dying lamp;
While o'er fond Fancy's pale perspective flitting,
  Successive forms their fleet ideas stamp.
Yet say, is bliss upon his brow impress'd? [live?
  Does jocund Health in Thought's still mansion
Lo, the cold dews that on his temples rest,
  That short quick sigh — their sad responses give

And canst thou rob a poet of his song;
  Snatch from the bard his trivial meed of praise?
Small are his gains, nor does he hold them long;
  Then leave, oh, leave him to enjoy his lays
While yet he lives — for to his merits just,
  Though future ages join his fame to raise,
Will the loud trump awake his cold unheeding dust?

. . . . . .

## LINES.

Yes, my stray steps have wander'd, wander'd far
From thee, and long, heart-soothing Poesy!
And many a flower, which in the passing time
My heart hath register'd, nipp'd by the chill

Of undeserved neglect, hath shrunk and died.
Heart-soothing Poesy! Though thou hast ceased
To hover o'er the many-voiced strings
Of my long silent lyre, yet thou canst still
Call the warm tear from its thrice hallow'd cell,
And with recalled images of bliss
Warm my reluctant heart. Yes, I would throw,
Once more would throw a quick and hurried hand
O'er the responding chords. It hath not ceased —
It cannot, will not cease; the heavenly warmth
Plays round my heart, and mantles o'er my cheek;
Still, though unbidden, plays. Fair Poesy!
The summer and the spring, the wind and rain,
Sunshine and storm, with various interchange,
Have mark'd full many a day, and week, and month,
Since by dark wood, or hamlet far retired,
Spell-struck, with thee I loiter'd. Sorceress!
I cannot burst thy bonds. It is but lift
Thy blue eyes to that deep-bespangled vault,
Wreathe thy enchanted tresses round thine arm,
And mutter some obscure and charmed rhyme,
And I could follow thee, on thy night's work,
Up to the regions of thrice chasten'd fire,
Or, in the caverns of the ocean flood,
Thrid the light mazes of thy volant foot.
Yet other duties call me, and mine ear
Must turn away from the high minstrelsy
Of thy soul-trancing harp, unwillingly
Must turn away; there are severer strains
(And surely they are sweet as ever smote

The ear of spirit, from this mortal coil
Released and disembodied), there are strains
Forbid to all, save those whom solemn thought,
Through the probation of revolving years,
And mighty converse with the spirit of truth,
Have purged and purified. To these my soul
Aspireth; and to this sublimer end
I gird myself, and climb the toilsome steep
With patient expectation. Yea, sometimes
Foretaste of bliss rewards me; and sometimes
Spirits unseen upon my footsteps wait,
And minister strange music, which doth seem
Now near, now distant, now on high, now low,
Then swelling from all sides, with bliss complete,
And full fruition filling all the soul.
Surely such ministry, though rare, may soothe
The steep ascent, and cheat the lassitude
Of toil; and but that my fond heart
Reverts to day-dreams of the summer gone,
When by clear fountain, or embower'd brake,
I lay a listless muser, prizing, far
Above all other lore, the poet's theme;
But for such recollections I could brace
My stubborn spirit for the arduous path
Of science unregretting; eye afar
Philosophy upon her steepest height,
And with bold step and resolute attempt
Pursue her to the innermost recess,
Where throned in light she sits, the Queen of Truth.

## THE PROSTITUTE.

### DACTYLICS.

WOMAN of weeping eye, ah! for thy wretched lot,
Putting on smiles to lure the lewd passenger,
Smiling while anguish gnaws at thy heavy heart;

Sad is thy chance, thou daughter of misery,
Vice and disease are wearing thee fast away,
While the unfeeling ones sport with thy sufferings.

Destined to pamper the vicious one's appetite;
Spurned by the beings who lured thee from innocence;
Sinking unnoticed in sorrow and indigence;

Thou hast no friends, for they with thy virtue fled;
Thou art an outcast from house and from happiness;
Wandering alone on the wide world's unfeeling stage!

Daughter of misery, sad is thy prospect here;
Thou hast no friend to soothe down the bed of death;
None after thee inquires with solicitude;

Famine and fell disease shortly will wear thee down,
Yet thou hast still to brave often the winter's wind,
Loathsome to those thou wouldst court with thine hollow eyes.

Soon thou wilt sink into death's silent slumbering,
And not a tear shall fall on thy early grave,
Nor shall a single stone tell where thy bones are laid.

Once wert thou happy — thou wert once innocent;
But the seducer beguiled thee in artlessness,
Then he abandoned thee unto thine infamy.

Now he perhaps is reclined on a bed of down:
But if a wretch like him sleeps in security,
God of the red right arm! where is thy thunder-bolt?

# ODES.

## TO MY LYRE.

THOU simple Lyre! thy music wild
  Has served to charm the weary hour,
And many a lonely night has 'guiled,
When even pain has own'd, and smiled,
  Its fascinating power.

Yet, O my Lyre! the busy crowd
  Will little heed thy simple tones;
Them mightier minstrel's harping loud
Engross, — and thou and I must shroud
  Where dark oblivion 'thrones.

No hand, thy diapason o'er,
  Well skill'd I throw with sweep sublime;
For me, no academic lore
Has taught the solemn strain to pour,
  Or build the polish'd rhyme.

Yet thou to sylvan themes canst soar;
  Thou know'st to charm the woodland train;
The rustic swains believe thy power
Can hush the wild winds when they roar,
  And still the billowy main.

These honours, Lyre, we yet may keep,
I, still unknown, may live with thee,
And gentle zephyr's wing will sweep
Thy solemn string, where low I sleep,
Beneath the alder tree.

This little dirge will please me more
Than the full requiem's swelling peal;
I'd rather than that crowds should sigh
For me, that from some kindred eye
The trickling tear should steal.

Yet dear to me the wreath of bay,
Perhaps from me debarr'd;
And dear to me the classic zone,
Which, snatch'd from learning's labour'd throne,
Adorns the accepted bard.

And O! if yet 'twere mine to dwell
Where Cam or Isis winds along,
Perchance, inspired with ardour chaste,
I yet might call the ear of taste
To listen to my song.

Oh! then, my little friend, thy style
I'd change to happier lays,
Oh! then the cloister'd glooms should smile,
And through the long, the fretted aisle
Should swell the note of praise.

## TO AN EARLY PRIMROSE.

Mild offspring of a dark and sullen sire!
Whose modest form, so delicately fine,
Was nursed in whirling storms,
And cradled in the winds.

Thee when young spring first question'd winter's sway,
And dared the sturdy blusterer to the fight,
Thee on this bank he threw
To mark his victory.

In this low vale, the promise of the year,
Serene thou openest to the nipping gale,
Unnoticed and alone,
Thy tender elegance.

So virtue blooms, brought forth amid the storms
Of chill adversity, in some lone walk
Of life she rears her head,
Obscure and unobserved;

While every bleaching breeze that on her blows
Chastens her spotless purity of breast,
And hardens her to bear
Serene the ills of life.

## ODE ADDRESSED TO H. FUSELI, Esq. R. A

### ON SEEING ENGRAVINGS FROM HIS DESIGNS.

Mighty magician! who on Torneo's brow,
  When sullen tempests wrap the throne of night,
  Art wont to sit and catch the gleam of light
That shoots athwart the gloom opaque below;
And listen to the distant death-shriek long
  From lonely mariner foundering in the deep,
  Which rises slowly up the rocky steep,
While the weird sisters weave the horrid song:
  Or, when along the liquid sky
  Serenely chant the orbs on high,
  Dost love to sit in musing trance,
  And mark the northern meteor's dance
  (While far below the fitful oar
  Flings its faint pauses on the steepy shore),
  And list the music of the breeze,
  That sweeps by fits the bending seas;
  And often bears with sudden swell
  The shipwreck'd sailor's funeral knell,
  By the spirits sung, who keep
  Their night-watch on the treacherous deep,
  And guide the wakeful helmsman's eye
  Tc Helice in northern sky;
  And there upon the rock reclined
  With mighty visions fill'st the mind,

Such as bound in magic spell
Him* who grasp'd the gates of Hell,
And, bursting Pluto's dark domain,
Held to the day the terrors of his reign.

Genius of Horror and romantic awe,
Whose eye explores the secrets of the deep,
Whose power can bid the rebel fluids creep,
Can force the inmost soul to own its law;
Who shall now, sublimest spirit,
Who shall now thy wand inherit,
From him† thy darling child who best
Thy shuddering images express'd?
Sullen of soul, and stern, and proud,
His gloomy spirit spurn'd the crowd,
And now he lays his aching head
In the dark mansion of the silent dead.

Mighty magician! long thy wand has lain
Buried beneath the unfathomable deep;
And oh! for ever must its efforts sleep,
May none the mystic sceptre e'er regain?
Oh, yes, 'tis his! Thy other son!
He throws thy dark-wrought tunic on,
Fuesslin waves thy wand, — again they rise,
Again thy wildering forms salute our ravish'd [eyes.
Him didst thou cradle on the dizzy steep
Where round his head the vollied lightnings flung,
And the loud winds that round his pillow rung
Woo'd the stern infant to the arms of sleep.

* Dante. † Ibid.

Or on the highest top of Teneriffe
Seated the fearless boy, and bade him look
Where far below the weather-beaten skiff
On the gulf bottom of the ocean strook.
Thou mark'dst him drink with ruthless ear
The death-sob, and, disdaining rest,
Thou saw'st how danger fired his breast,
And in his young hand couch'd the visionary spear.
Then, Superstition, at thy call,
She bore the boy to Odin's Hall,
And set before his awe-struck sight
The savage feast and spectred fight;
And summon'd from his mountain tomb
The ghastly warrior son of gloom,
His fabled runic rhymes to sing,
While fierce Hresvelger flapp'd his wing;
Thou show'dst the trains the shepherd sees,
Laid on the stormy Hebrides,
Which on the mists of evening gleam,
Or crowd the foaming desert stream;
Lastly her storied hand she waves,
And lays him in Florentian caves;
There milder fables, lovelier themes,
Enwrap his soul in heavenly dreams,
There pity's lute arrests his ear,
And draws the half reluctant tear;
And now at noon of night he roves
Along the embowering moonlight groves,
And as from many a cavern'd dell
The hollow wind is heard to swell,

He thinks some troubled spirit sighs,
And as upon the turf he lies,
Where sleeps the silent beam of night,
He sees below the gliding sprite,
And hears in Fancy's organs sound
Aërial music warbling round.

Taste lastly comes and smooths the whole,
And breathes her polish o'er his soul;
Glowing with wild, yet chasten'd heat,
The wondrous work is now complete.

The Poet dreams: — The shadow flies,
And fainting fast its image dies.
But lo! the Painter's magic force
Arrests the phantom's fleeting course;
It lives — it lives — the canvas glows,
And tenfold vigour o'er it flows.
The Bard beholds the work achieved,
And as he sees the shadow rise
Sublime before his wondering eyes,
Starts at the image his own mind conceived.

---

## TO THE EARL OF CARLISLE, K. G.

I. 1.

Retired, remote from human noise,
An humble Poet dwelt serene;
His lot was lowly, yet his joys
Were manifold, I ween.

He laid him by the brawling brook
At eventide to ruminate,
He watch'd the swallow skimming round,
And mused, in reverie profound,
On wayward man's unhappy state,
And ponder'd much, and paused on deeds of ancient date.

II. 1.

"Oh, 'twas not always thus," he cried,
"There was a time, when genius claim'd
Respect from even towering pride,
Nor hung her head ashamed:
But now to wealth alone we bow,
The titled and the rich alone
Are honour'd, while meek merit pines,
On penury's wretched couch reclines,
Unheeded in his dying moan,
As, overwhelm'd with want and woe, he sinks unknown.

III. 1.

"Yet was the muse not always seen
In poverty's dejected mien,
Not always did repining rue,
And misery her steps pursue.
Time was, when nobles thought their titles graced
By the sweet honours of poetic bays,
When Sidney sung his melting song,
When Sheffield join'd the harmonious throng,
And Lyttelton attuned to love his lays.

Those days are gone — alas, for ever gone!
  No more our nobles love to grace
Their brows with anadems, by genius won,
  But arrogantly deem the muse as base;
How differently thought the sires of this degenerate
    race!"

I. 2.

Thus sang the minstrel: — still at eve
  The upland's woody shades among
In broken measures did he grieve,
  With solitary song.
And still his shame was aye the same,
  Neglect had stung him to the core;
And he with pensive joy did love
To seek the still congenial grove,
  And muse on all his sorrows o'er,
And vow that he would join the abjured world no
    more.

II. 2.

But human vows, how frail they be!
  Fame brought Carlisle unto his view,
And all amazed, he thought to see
  The Augustan age anew.
Fill'd with wild rapture, up he rose,
No more he ponders on the woes
Which erst he felt that forward goes,
  Regrets he'd sunk in impotence,
And hails the ideal day of virtuous eminence.

III. 2.

Ah! silly man, yet smarting sore
With ills which in the world he bore,
Again on futile hope to rest,
An unsubstantial prop at best,
And not to know one swallow makes no summer!
Ah! soon he'll find the brilliant gleam,
Which flash'd across the hemisphere,
Illumining the darkness there,
Was but a single solitary beam,
While all around remain'd in custom'd night.
Still leaden ignorance reigns serene,
In the false court's delusive height,
And only one Carlisle is seen
To illume the heavy gloom with pure and steady light.

---

## TO CONTEMPLATION.

Come, pensive sage, who lovest to dwell
In some retired Lapponian cell,
Where, far from noise and riot rude,
Resides sequester'd solitude.
Come, and o'er my longing soul
Throw thy dark and russet stole,
And open to my duteous eyes
The volume of thy mysteries.

I will meet thee on the hill,
Where, with printless footsteps still,
The morning in her buskin gray
Springs upon her eastern way;
While the frolic zephyrs stir,
Playing with the gossamer,
And, on ruder pinions borne,
Shake the dewdrops from the thorn.
There, as o'er the fields we pass,
Brushing with hasty feet the grass,
We will startle from her nest
The lively lark with speckled breast,
And hear the floating clouds among
Her gale-transported matin song,
Or on the upland stile, embower'd
With fragrant hawthorn snowy flower'd,
Will sauntering sit, and listen still
To the herdsman's oaten quill,
Wafted from the plain below;
Or the heifer's frequent low;
Or the milkmaid in the grove,
Singing of one that died for love.
Or when the noontide heats oppress,
We will seek the dark recess,
Where, in the embower'd translucent stream,
The cattle shun the sultry beam,
And o'er us on the marge reclined,
The drowsy fly her horn shall wind,
While echo, from her ancient oak,
Shall answer to the woodman's stroke;

Or the little peasant's song,
Wandering lone the glens among,
His artless lip with berries dyed,
And feet through ragged shoes descried.
But oh! when evening's virgin queen
Sits on her fringed throne serene,
And mingling whispers rising near
Steal on the still reposing ear;
While distant brooks decaying round,
Augment the mix'd dissolving sound,
And the zephyr flitting by
Whispers mystic harmony,
We will seek the woody lane,
By the hamlet, on the plain,
Where the weary rustic nigh
Shall whistle his wild melody,
And the croaking wicket oft
Shall echo from the neighbouring croft;
And as we trace the green path lone,
With moss and rank weeds overgrown,
We will muse on pensive lore,
Till the full soul, brimming o'er,
Shall in our upturn'd eyes appear,
Embodied in a quivering tear.
Or else, serenely silent, sit
By the brawling rivulet,
Which on its calm unruffled breast
Rears the old mossy arch impress'd,
That clasps its secret stream of glass,
Half hid in shrubs and waving grass,

The wood-nympth's lone secure retreat,
Unpress'd by fawn or sylvan's feet,
We'll watch in eve's ethereal braid
The rich vermilion slowly fade;
Or catch, faint twinkling from afar
The first glimpse of the eastern star;
Fair vesper, mildest lamp of light,
That heralds in imperial night:
Meanwhile, upon our wondering ear,
Shall rise, though low, yet sweetly clear,
The distant sounds of pastoral lute,
Invoking soft the sober suit
Of dimmest darkness — fitting well
With love, or sorrow's pensive spell,
(So erst did music's silver tone
Wake slumbering chaos on his throne).
And haply then, with sudden swell,
Shall roar the distant curfew bell,
While in the castle's mouldering tower
The hooting owl is heard to pour
Her melancholy song, and scare
Dull silence brooding in the air.
Meanwhile her dusk and slumbering car
Black-suited night drives on from far,
And Cynthia, 'merging from her rear,
Arrests the waxing darkness drear,
And summons to her silent call,
Sweeping, in their airy pall,
The unshrived ghosts, in fairy trance,
To join her moonshine morris-dance;

While around the mystic ring
The shadowy shapes elastic spring,
Then with a passing shriek they fly,
Wrapt in mists, along the sky,
And oft are by the shepherd seen
In his lone night-watch on the green.
Then, hermit, let us turn our feet
To the low abbey's still retreat,
Embower'd in the distant glen,
Far from the haunts of busy men,
Where as we sit upon the tomb,
The glowworm's light may gild the gloom,
And show to fancy's saddest eye
Where some lost hero's ashes lie.
And oh, as through the mouldering arch,
With ivy fill'd and weeping larch,
The night gale whispers sadly clear,
Speaking dear things to fancy's ear,
We'll hold communion with the shade
Of some deep wailing, ruin'd maid—
Or call the ghost of Spenser down,
To tell of woe and fortune's frown;
And bid us cast the eye of hope
Beyond this bad world's narrow scope.
Or if these joys, to us denied,
To linger by the forest's side;
Or in the meadow, or the wood,
Or by the lone, romantic flood;
Let us in the busy town,
When sleep's dull streams the people drown,

Far from drowsy pillows flee,
And turn the church's massy key;
Then, as through the painted glass
The moon's faint beams obscurely pass,
And darkly on the trophied wall
Her faint, ambiguous shadows fall,
Let us, while the faint winds wail
Through the long reluctant aisle,
As we pace with reverence meet,
Count the echoings of our feet,
While from the tombs, with confess'd breath,
Distinct responds the voice of death.
If thou, mild sage, wilt condescend
Thus on my footsteps to attend,
To thee my lonely lamp shall burn
By fallen Genius' sainted urn,
As o'er the scroll of Time I pore,
And sagely spell of ancient lore,
Till I can rightly guess of all
That Plato could to memory call,
And scan the formless views of things;
Or, with old Egypt's fetter'd kings,
Arrange the mystic trains that shine
In night's high philosophic mine;
And to thy name shall e'er belong
The honours of undying song.

## TO THE GENIUS OF ROMANCE.

OH! thou who, in my early youth,
When fancy wore the garb of truth,
Wert wont to win my infant feet
To some retired, deep fabled seat,
Where, by the brooklet's secret tide,
The midnight ghost was known to glide;
Or lay me in some lonely glade,
In native Sherwood's forest shade,
Where Robin Hood, the outlaw bold,
Was wont his sylvan courts to hold;
And there, as musing deep I lay,
Would steal my little soul away,
And all my pictures represent,
Of siege and solemn tournament;
Or bear me to the magic scene,
Where, clad in greaves and gabardine,
The warrior knight of chivalry
Made many a fierce enchanter flee;
And bore the high-born dame away,
Long held the fell magician's prey.
Or oft would tell the shuddering tale
Of murders, and of goblins pale,
Haunting the guilty baron's side
(Whose floors with secret blood were dyed),
Which o'er the vaulted corridor
On stormy nights was heard to roar,

By old domestic, waken'd wide
By the angry winds that chide:
Or else the mystic tale would tell
Of Greensleeve, or of Blue-Beard fell.

. . . . . .

---

## TO MIDNIGHT.

SEASON of general rest, whose solemn still
Strikes to the trembling heart a fearful chill,
   But speaks to philosophic souls delight;
Thee do I hail, as at my casement high,
My candle waning melancholy by,
   I sit and taste the holy calm of night.

Yon pensive orb, that through the ether sails,
And gilds the misty shadows of the vales,
   Hanging in thy dull rear her vestal flame;
To her, while all around in sleep recline,
Wakeful I raise my orisons divine,
   And sing the gentle honours of her name;

While Fancy lone o'er me, her votary, bends,
To lift my soul her fairy visions sends,
   And pours upon my ear her thrilling song,
And Superstition's gentle terrors come,—
See, see yon dim ghost gliding through the gloom!
   See round yon churchyard elm what spectres
      throng!

Meanwhile I tune, to some romantic lay,
My flageolet — and as I pensive play,
The sweet notes echo o'er the mountain scene:
The traveller late journeying o'er the moors,
Hears them aghast, — (while still the dull owl pours
Her hollow screams each dreary pause between).

Till in the lonely tower he spies the light,
Now faintly flashing on the glooms of night,
Where I, poor muser, my lone vigils keep,
And, 'mid the dreary solitude serene,
Cast a much-meaning glance upon the scene,
And raise my mournful eye to Heaven, and weep.

---

## TO THOUGHT.

### WRITTEN AT MIDNIGHT.

Hence, away, vindictive thought;
Thy pictures are of pain;
The visions through thy dark eye caught,
They with no gentle charms are fraught,
So pr'y thee back again.
I would not weep,
I wish to sleep,
Then why, thou busy foe, with me thy vigils keep?

Why dost o'er bed and couch recline?
Is this thy new delight?
Pale visitant, it is not thine
To keep thy sentry through the mine,

The dark vault of the night:
'T is thine to die,
While o'er the eye
The dews of slumber press, and waking sorrows fly.

Go thou, and bide with him who guides
His bark through lonely seas;
And as reclining on his helm,
Sadly he marks the starry realm,
To him thou mayst bring ease:
But thou to me
Art misery, [my pillow flee.
So pr'ythee, pr'ythee, plume thy wings, and from

And, memory, pray what art thou?
Art thou of pleasure born?
Does bliss untainted from thee flow?
The rose that gems thy pensive brow,
Is it without a thorn?
With all thy smiles,
And witching wiles, [defiles.
Yet not unfrequent bitterness thy mournful sway

The drowsy night-watch has forgot
To call the solemn hour;
Lull'd by the winds, he slumbers deep,
While I in vain, capricious sleep,
Invoke thy tardy power;
And restless lie,
With unclosed eye,
And count the tedious hours as slow they minute by.

## GENIUS.

### AN ODE.

I. 1.

Many there be, who, through the vale of life,
With velvet pace, unnoticed, softly go,
While jarring discord's inharmonious strife
Awakes them not to woe.
By them unheeded, carking care,
Green-eyed grief and dull despair;
Smoothly they pursue their way,
With even tenor and with equal breath,
Alike through cloudy and through sunny day,
Then sink in peace to death.

II. 1.

But, ah! a few there be whom griefs devour,
And weeping woe, and disappointment keen,
Repining penury, and sorrow sour,
And self-consuming spleen.
And these are Genius' favourites: these
Know the thought-throned mind to please,
And from her fleshy seat to draw
To realms where Fancy's golden orbits roll,
Disdaining all but 'wildering rapture's law,
The captivated soul.

III. 1.

Genius, from thy starry throne,
High above the burning zone,
In radiant robe of light array'd,
Oh! hear the plaint by thy sad favourite made,
His melancholy moan.
He tells of scorn, he tells of broken vows,
Of sleepless nights, of anguish-ridden days,
Pangs that his sensibility uprouse
To curse his being and his thirst for praise.
Thou gavest to him with treble force to feel
The sting of keen neglect, the rich man's scorn,
And what o'er all does in his soul preside
Predominant, and tempers him to steel,
His high indignant pride.

I. 2.

Lament not ye, who humbly steal through life,
That Genius visits not your lowly shed;
For, ah, what woes and sorrows ever rife
Distract his hapless head!
For him awaits no balmy sleep,
He wakes all night, and wakes to weep;
Or by his lonely lamp he sits
At solemn midnight, when the peasant sleeps,
In feverish study, and in moody fits
His mournful vigils keeps.

II. 2.

And, oh! for what consumes his watchful oil?
For what does thus he waste life's fleeting
'Tis for neglect and penury he doth toil, [breath?
'Tis for untimely death.
Lo! where dejected pale he lies,
Despair depicted in his eyes,
He feels the vital flame decrease,
He sees the grave wide yawning for its prey,
Without a friend to soothe his soul to peace,
And cheer the expiring ray.

III. 2.

By Sulmo's bard of mournful fame,
By gentle Otway's magic name,
By him, the youth, who smiled at death,
And rashly dared to stop his vital breath,
Will I thy pangs proclaim;
For still to misery closely thou 'rt allied,
Though gaudy pageants glitter by thy side,
And far resounding Fame.
What though to thee the dazzled millions bow,
And to thy posthumous merit bend them low;
Though unto thee the monarch looks with awe,
And thou at thy flash'd car dost nations draw,
Yet, ah! unseen behind thee fly
Corroding Anguish, soul-subduing Pain,
And Discontent that clouds the fairest sky,
A melancholy train.

Yes, Genius, thee a thousand cares await,
Mocking thy derided state;
Thee chill Adversity will still attend,
Before whose face flies fast the summer's friend
And leaves thee all forlorn;
While leaden Ignorance rears her head and laughs,
And fat Stupidity shakes his jolly sides,
And while the cup of affluence he quaffs
With bee-eyed Wisdom, Genius derides,
Who toils, and every hardship doth outbrave,
To gain the meed of praise when he is mouldering in his grave.

---

## FRAGMENT OF AN ODE TO THE MOON.

Mild orb, who floatest through the realm of night,
A pathless wanderer o'er a lonely wild,
Welcome to me thy soft and pensive light,
Which oft in childhood my lone thoughts beguiled.
Now doubly dear as o'er my silent seat,
Nocturnal study's still retreat,
It casts a mournful melancholy gleam,
And through my lofty casement weaves,
Dim through the vine's encircling leaves,
An intermingled beam.

These feverish dews that on my temples hang,
 This quivering lip, these eyes of dying flame;
These the dread signs of many a secret pang,
 These are the meed of him who pants for fame!
Pale Moon, from thoughts like these divert my soul;
 Lowly I kneel before thy shrine on high;
My lamp expires; — beneath thy mild control
These restless dreams are ever wont to fly.

Come, kindred mourner, in my breast
Soothe these discordant tones to rest,
  And breathe the soul of peace;
Mild visitor, I feel thee here,
It is not pain that brings this tear,
  For thou hast bid it cease.
Oh! many a year has pass'd away
Since I, beneath thy fairy ray,
  Attuned my infant reed;
When wilt thou, Time, those days restore,
Those happy moments now no more —

. . . . . . . .

When on the lake's damp marge I lay,
 And mark'd the northern meteor's dance,
Bland Hope and Fancy, ye were there
 To inspirate my trance.
  Twin sisters, faintly now ye deign
Your magic sweets on me to shed,
In vain your powers are now essay'd
  To chase superior pain.

And art thou fled, thou welcome orb!
  So swiftly pleasure flies,
So to mankind, in darkness lost,
  The beam of ardour dies.
Wan Moon, thy nightly task is done,
And now, encurtain'd in the main,
    Thou sinkest into rest;
But I, in vain, on thorny bed
Shall woo the god of soft repose —

. . . . . . .

---

## TO THE MUSE.

### WRITTEN AT THE AGE OF FOURTEEN.

  Ill-fated maid, in whose unhappy train
Chill poverty and misery are seen,
  Anguish and discontent, the unhappy bane
Of life, and blackener of each brighter scene.
  Why to thy votaries dost thou give to feel
So keenly all the scorns — the jeers of life?
Why not endow them to endure the strife
  With apathy's invulnerable steel,
  Of self-content and ease, each torturing wound to
      heal?

  Ah! who would taste your self-deluding joys,
That lure the unwary to a wretched doom,
  That bid fair views and flattering hopes arise,
Then hurl them headlong to a lasting tomb?
  What is the charm which leads thy victims on

To persevere in paths that lead to woe?
What can induce them in that route to go,
  In which innumerous before have gone,
  And died in misery poor and woe-begone?

  Yet can I ask what charms in thee are found;
I, who have drunk from thine ethereal rill,
  And tasted all the pleasures that abound
Upon Parnassus' loved Aonian hill?
  I, through whose soul the Muse's strains aye thrill!
Oh! I do feel the spell with which I'm tied;
  And though our annals fearful stories tell,
How Savage languish'd, and how Otway died,
Yet must I persevere, let whate'er will betide.

---

## TO LOVE.

Why should I blush to own I love?
'Tis Love that rules the realms above.
Why should I blush to say to all,
That Virtue holds my heart in thrall?

Why should I seek the thickest shade,
Lest Love's dear secret be betray'd?
Why the stern brow deceitful move,
When I am languishing with love?

Is it weakness thus to dwell
On passion that I dare not tell?
Such weakness I would ever prove;
'Tis painful, though 'tis sweet to love.

## ON WHIT-MONDAY.

Hark! how the merry bells ring jocund round,
And now they die upon the veering breeze
Anon they thunder loud
Full on the musing ear.

Wafted in varying cadence, by the shore
Of the still twinkling river, they bespeak
A day of jubilee,
An ancient holiday.

And lo! the rural revels are begun,
And gaily echoing to the laughing sky,
On the smooth shaven green
Resounds the voice of Mirth.

Alas! regardless of the tongue of Fate,
That tells them 'tis but as an hour since they
Who now are in their graves
Kept up the Whitsun dance.

And that another hour, and they must fall
Like those who went before, and sleep as still
Beneath the silent sod,
A cold and cheerless sleep.

Yet why should thoughts like these intrude to scare
The vagrant Happiness, when she will deign
To smile upon us here,
A transient visitor?

Mortals! be gladsome while ye have the power,
And laugh and seize the glittering lapse of joy;
In time the bell will toll
That warns ye to your graves.

I to the woodland solitude will bend
My lonesome way — where Mirth's obstreperous shout
Shall not intrude to break
The meditative hour.

There will I ponder on the state of man,
Joyless and sad of heart, and consecrate
This day of jubilee
To sad reflection's shrine;

And I will cast my fond eye far beyond
This world of care, to where the steeple loud
Shall rock above the sod,
Where I shall sleep in peace.

## TO THE WIND, AT MIDNIGHT.

NOT unfamiliar to mine ear,
Blasts of the night! ye howl as now
My shuddering casement loud
With fitful force ye beat.

Mine ear has dwelt in silent awe,
The howling sweep, the sudden rush;
And when the passing gale
Pour'd deep the hollow dirge.

. . . . . . . .

## TO THE HARVEST MOON.

Cum ruit imbriferum ver:
Spicea jam campis cum messis inhorruit, et cum
Frumenta in viridi stipula lactentia turgent.

Cuncta tibi Cererem pubes agrestis adoret.
VIRGIL.

MOON of Harvest, herald mild
Of plenty rustic labour's child,
Hail! oh hail! I greet thy beam,
As soft it trembles o'er the stream,
And gilds the straw-thatch'd hamlet wide,
Where Innocence and Peace reside!
'T is thou that gladd'st with joy the rustic throng,
Promptest the tripping dance, the exhilarating song

Moon of Harvest, I do love
O'er the uplands now to rove,
While thy modest ray serene
Gilds the wide surrounding scene;
And to watch thee riding high
In the blue vault of the sky,
Where no thin vapour intercepts thy ray,
But in unclouded majesty thou walkest on thy way.

Pleasing 'tis, oh! modest Moon!
Now the night is at her noon,
'Neath thy sway to musing lie,
While around the zephyrs sigh,
Fanning soft the sun-tann'd wheat,
Ripen'd by the summer's heat;
Picturing all the rustic's joy
When boundless plenty greets his eye,
And thinking soon,
Oh, modest Moon!
How many a female eye will roam
Along the road,
To see the load,
The last dear load of harvest home.

Storms and tempests, floods and rains,
Stern despoilers of the plains,
Hence, away, the season flee,
Foes to light-heart jollity:
May no winds careering high
Drive the clouds along the sky,

But may all nature smile with aspect boon,
When in the heavens thou show'st thy face, oh
Harvest Moon!

'Neath yon lowly roof he lies,
The husbandman, with deep-seal'd eyes:
He dreams of crowded barns, and round
The yard he hears the flail resound;
Oh! may no hurricane destroy
His visionary views of joy!
God of the winds! oh, hear his humble prayer,
And while the Moon of Harvest shines, thy bluster-
ing whirlwind spare.

Sons of luxury, to you
Leave I sleep's dull power to woo;
Press ye still the downy bed,
While feverish dreams surround your head;
I will seek the woodland glade,
Penetrate the thickest shade,
Wrapp'd in contemplation's dreams,
Musing high on holy themes,
While on the gale
Shall softly sail
The nightingale's enchanting tune,
And oft my eyes
Shall grateful rise
To thee, the modest Harvest Moon!

## TO THE HERB ROSEMARY.*

Sweet scented flower! who art wont to bloom
On January's front severe,
And o'er the wintry desert drear
To waft thy waste perfume!
Come, thou shalt form my nosegay now,
And I will bind thee round my brow;
And as I twine the mournful wreath,
I'll weave a melancholy song;
And sweet the strain shall be, and long,
The melody of death.

Come, funeral flower! who lovest to dwell
With the pale corse in lonely tomb,
And throw across the desert gloom
A sweet decaying smell.
Come, press my lips, and lie with me
Beneath the lowly alder tree,
And we will sleep a pleasant sleep,
And not a care shall dare intrude
To break the marble solitude,
So peaceful and so deep.

And hark! the wind god, as he flies,
Moans hollow in the forest trees,
And sailing on the gusty breeze,

* The Rosemary buds in January. It is the flower commonly put in the coffins of the dead.

Mysterious music dies.
Sweet flower! that requiem wild is mine,
It warns me to the lonely shrine,
The cold turf altar of the dead:
My grave shall be in yon lone spot,
Where as I lie, by all forgot,
A dying fragrance thou wilt o'er my ashes shed.

---

## TO THE MORNING.

### WRITTEN DURING ILLNESS.

Beams of the daybreak faint! I hail
Your dubious hues, as on the robe
Of night, which wraps the slumbering globe,
I mark your traces pale.
Tired with the taper's sickly light,
And with the wearying, number'd night,
I hail the streaks of morn divine:
And lo! they break between the dewy wreaths
That round my rural casement twine;
The fresh gale o'er the green lawn breathes,
It fans my feverish brow, — it calms the mental strife,
And cheerily re-illumes the lambent flame of life.

The lark has her gay song begun,
She leaves her grassy nest,
And soars till the unrisen sun
Gleams on her speckled breast.

Now let me leave my restless bed,
And o'er the spangled uplands tread;
Now through the custom'd wood walk wend;
By many a green lane lies my way,
Where high o'er head the wild briers bend,
Till on the mountain's summit gray,
I sit me down, and mark the glorious dawn of day.

Oh Heaven! the soft refreshing gale
It breathes into my breast!
My sunk eye gleams; my cheek, so pale,
Is with new colours dress'd.

Blithe Health! thou soul of life and ease!
Come thou, too, on the balmy breeze,
Invigorate my frame:
I'll join with thee the buskin'd chase,
With thee the distant clime will trace
Beyond those clouds of flame.

Above, below, what charms unfold
In all the varied view!
Before me all is burnish'd gold,
Behind the twilight's hue.
The mists which on old Night await,
Far to the west they hold their state,
They shun the clear blue face of Morn;
Along the fine cerulean sky
The fleecy clouds successive fly,
While bright prismatic beams their shadowy folds [adorn.

And hark! the thatcher has begun
  His whistle on the eaves,
And oft the hedger's bill is heard
  Among the rustling leaves.
The slow team creaks upon the road,
  The noisy whip resounds,
The driver's voice, his carol blithe,
The mower's stroke, his whetting scythe
  Mix with the morning's sounds.

Who would not rather take his seat
  Beneath these clumps of trees,
The early dawn of day to greet,
  And catch the healthy breeze,
Than on the silken couch of Sloth
  Luxurious to lie;
Who would not from life's dreary waste
Snatch, when he could, with eager haste,
  An interval of joy!

To him who simply thus recounts
  The morning's pleasures o'er,
Fate dooms, ere long, the scene must close
  To ope on him no more.
Yet Morning! unrepining still,
  He'll greet thy beams awhile;
And surely thou, when o'er his grave
Solemn the whispering willows wave,
  Wilt sweetly on him smile:
And the pale glowworm's pensive light [night.
Will guide his ghostly walks in the drear moonless

## ON DISAPPOINTMENT.

Come, Disappointment, come!
Not in thy terrors clad:
Come, in thy meekest, saddest guise;
Thy chastening rod but terrifies
The restless and the bad.
But I recline
Beneath thy shrine, [twine.
And round my brow resign'd thy peaceful cypress

Though Fancy flies away
Before thy hollow tread,
Yet Meditation, in her cell,
Hears with faint eye the lingering knell
That tells her hopes are dead;
And though the tear
By chance appear,
Yet she can smile, and say, My all was not laid here.

Come, Disappointment, come!
Though from Hope's summit hurl'd,
Still, rigid Nurse, thou art forgiven,
For thou severe wert sent from heaven
To wean me from the world;
To turn my eye
From vanity,
And point to scenes of bliss that never, never die.

What is this passing scene?
A peevish April day!
A little sun — a little rain,
And then night sweeps along the plain,
And all things fade away.
Man (soon discuss'd)
Yields up his trust,
And all his hopes and fears lie with him in the dust.

Oh, what is Beauty's power?
It flourishes and dies;
Will the cold earth its silence break,
To tell how soft, how smooth a cheek
Beneath its surface lies?
Mute, mute is all
O'er Beauty's fall;
Her praise resounds no more when mantled in her [pall.

The most beloved on earth
Not long survives to-day;
So music past is obsolete,
And yet 'twas sweet, 'twas passing sweet,
But now 'tis gone away.
Thus does the shade
In memory fade,
When in forsaken tomb the form beloved is laid.

Then since this world is vain,
And volatile, and fleet,

Why should I lay up earthly joys,
Where rust corrupts, and moth destroys,
And cares and sorrows eat?
Why fly from ill
With anxious skill,
When soon this hand will freeze, this throbbing heart be still.

Come, Disappointment, come!
Thou art not stern to me;
Sad Monitress! I own thy sway,
A votary sad in early day,
I bend my knee to thee.
From sun to sun
My race will run,
I only bow, and say, My God, thy will be done!

On another paper are a few lines, written probably in the freshness of his disappointment.

I dream no more — the vision flies away,
And Disappointment . . . .
There fell my hopes — I lost my all in this,
My cherish'd all of visionary bliss.
Now hope farewell, farewell all joys below;
Now welcome sorrow, and now welcome woe.
Plunge me in glooms . . . .

## ON THE DEATH OF DERMODY THE POET.

CHILD of Misfortune! Offspring of the Muse!
Mark like the meteor's gleam his mad career;
With hollow cheeks and haggard eye,
Behold he shrieking passes by:
I see, I see him near:
That hollow scream, that deepening groan;
It rings upon mine ear.

Oh come, ye thoughtless, ye deluded youth,
Who clasp the syren pleasure to your breast,
Behold the wreck of genius here,
And drop, oh drop the silent tear
For Dermody at rest:
His fate is yours, then from your loins
Tear quick the silken vest.

Saw'st thou his dying bed! Saw'st thou his eye,
Once flashing fire, despair's dim tear distil;
How ghastly did it seem;
And then his dying scream:
Oh God! I hear it still:
It sounds upon my fainting sense,
It strikes with deathly chill.

Say, didst thou mark the brilliant poet's death;
  Saw'st thou an anxious father by his bed,
    Or pitying friends around him stand:
    Or didst thou see a mother's hand
      Support his languid head:
    Oh none of these — no friend o'er him
      The balm of pity shed.

Now come around, ye flippant sons of wealth,
  Sarcastic smile on genius fallen low;
    Now come around who pant for fame,
    And learn from hence, a poet's name
      Is purchased but by woe:
    And when ambition prompts to rise,
      Oh think of him below.

For me, poor moralizer, I will run,
  Dejected, to some solitary state:
    The muse has set her seal on me,
    She set her seal on Dermody,
      It is the seal of fate:
    In some lone spot my bones may lie,
      Secure from human hate.

Yet ere I go I'll drop one silent tear,
  Where lies unwept the poet's fallen head:
    May peace her banners o'er him wave;
    For me in my deserted grave
      No friend a tear shall shed:
    Yet may the lily and the rose
      Bloom on my grassy bed.

## SONNETS.

### SONNET TO THE RIVER TRENT.

WRITTEN ON RECOVERY FROM SICKNESS.

Once more, O Trent! along thy pebbly marge
  A pensive invalid, reduced and pale,
From the close sick-room newly set at large,
  Woos to his wan worn cheek the pleasant gale.
O! to his ear how musical the tale
  Which fills with joy the throstle's little throat!
And all the sounds which on the fresh breeze sail,
  How wildly novel on his senses float!
It was on this that many a sleepless night,
  As lone he watch'd the taper's sickly gleam,
And at his casement heard, with wild affright,
  The owl's dull wing, and melancholy scream,
On this he thought, this, this, his sole desire,
Thus once again to hear the warbling woodland choir.

---

### SONNET.

Give me a cottage on some Cambrian wild,
  Where far from cities I may spend my days;
And, by the beauties of the scene beguiled,
  May pity man's pursuits and shun his ways.
While on the rock I mark the browsing goat,

List to the mountain-torrent's distant noise,
Or the hoarse bittern's solitary note,
I shall not want the world's delusive joys;
But with my little scrip, my book, my lyre,
Shall think my lot complete, nor covet more;
And when, with time, shall wane the vital fire,
I'll raise my pillow on the desert shore,
And lay me down to rest where the wild wave
Shall make sweet music o'er my lonely grave.

---

## SONNET.*

### SUPPOSED TO HAVE BEEN ADDRESSED BY A FEMALE LUNATIC TO A LADY.

LADY, thou weepest for the Maniac's woe,
And thou art fair, and thou, like me, art young;
Oh! may thy bosom never, never know
The pangs with which my wretched heart is wrung.
I had a mother once — a brother too —
(Beneath yon yew my father rests his head:)
I had a lover once, and kind and true,
But mother, brother, lover, all are fled!
Yet, whence the tear which dims thy lovely eye?
Oh! gentle lady — not for me thus weep,
The green sod soon upon my breast will lie,
And soft and sound will be my peaceful sleep.
Go thou, and pluck the roses while they bloom —
My hopes lie buried in the silent tomb.

* This Quatorzain had its rise from an elegant Sonnet, "occasioned by seeing a young female Lunatic," written by Mrs. Lofft, and published in the Monthly Mirror.

## SONNET.

Supposed to be written by the unhappy Poet Dermody in a Storm, while on board a Ship in his Majesty's service.

Lo! o'er the welkin the tempestuous clouds
Successive fly, and the loud piping wind
Rocks the poor sea-boy on the dripping shrouds,
While the pale pilot, o'er the helm reclined,
Lists to the changeful storm: and as he plies
His wakeful task, he oft bethinks him, sad,
Of wife, and little home, and chubby lad,
And the half strangled tear bedews his eyes;
I, on the deck, musing on themes forlorn,
View the drear tempest, and the yawning deep,
Nought dreading in the green sea's caves to sleep,
For not for me shall wife or children mourn,
And the wild winds will ring my funeral knell,
Sweetly as solemn peal of pious passing-bell.

---

## SONNET. THE WINTER TRAVELLER.

God help thee, Traveller, on thy journey far;
The wind is bitter keen, — the snow o'erlays
The hidden pits, and dangerous hollow ways,
And darkness will involve thee. No kind star
To-night will guide thee, Traveller, — and the war
Of winds and elements on thy head will break,

And in thy agonizing ear the shriek
Of spirits howling on their stormy car
Will often ring appalling — I portend
A dismal night — and on my wakeful bed
Thoughts, Traveller, of thee will fill my head,
And him who rides where winds and waves contend,
And strives, rude cradled on the seas, to guide
His lonely bark through the tempestuous tide.

---

## SONNET.

BY CAPEL LOFFT, ESQ.

This Sonnet was addressed to the Author of this volume, and was occasioned by several little Quatorzains, misnomered Sonnets, which he published in the Monthly Mirror. He begs leave to return his thanks to the much respected writer, for the permission so politely granted to insert it here, and for the good opinion he has been pleased to express of his productions.

Ye whose aspirings court the muse of lays,
"Severest of those orders which belong,
Distinct and separate, to Delphic song,"
Why shun the sonnet's undulating maze?
And why its name, boast of Petrarchian days,
Assume, its rules disown'd? whom from the throng
The muse selects, their ear the charm obeys
Of its full harmony: — they fear to wrong

The sonnet, by adorning with a name
  Of that distinguish'd import, lays, though sweet,
  Yet not in magic texture taught to meet
Of that so varied and peculiar frame.
O think! to vindicate its genuine praise
Those it beseems, whose lyre a favouring impulse sways.

---

## SONNET.

RECANTATORY, IN REPLY TO THE FOREGOING ELEGANT ADMONITION.

Let the sublimer muse, who, wrapp'd in night,
  Rides on the raven pennons of the storm,
  Or o'er the field, with purple havoc warm,
Lashes her steeds, and sings along the fight;
Let her, whom more ferocious strains delight,
  Disdain the plaintive sonnet's little form,
  And scorn to its wild cadence to conform,
The impetuous tenor of her hardy flight.
But me, far lowest of the sylvan train,
  Who wake the wood-nymphs from the forest shade
  With wildest song; — me, much behoves thy aid
Of mingled melody, to grace my strain,
And give it power to please, as soft it flows
Through the smooth murmurs of thy frequent close.

## SONNET ON HEARING THE SOUNDS OF AN ÆOLIAN HARP.

So ravishingly soft upon the tide
  Of the infuriate gust, it did career,
  It might have soothed its rugged charioteer,
And sunk him to a zephyr; then it died,
Melting in melody; — and I descried,
  Borne to some wizard stream, the form appear
  Of Druid sage, who on the far-off ear
Pour'd his lone song, to which the surge replied:
Or thought I heard the hapless pilgrim's knell,
  Lost in some wild enchanted forest's bounds,
  By unseen beings sung; or are these sounds
Such as, 'tis said, at night are known to swell
By startled shepherd on the lonely heath,
Keeping his night-watch sad, portending death?

---

## SONNET.

What art thou, Mighty One! and where thy seat?
  Thou broodest on the calm that cheers the lands.
  And thou dost bear within thine awful hands
The rolling thunders and the lightnings fleet.
Stern on thy dark-wrought car of cloud and wind,
  Thou guidest the northern storm at night's dead
      noon,

Or, on the red wing of the fierce monsoon,
Disturb'st the sleeping giant of the Ind.
In the drear silence of the polar span
Dost thou repose? or in the solitude
Of sultry tracts, where the lone caravan
Hears nightly howl the tiger's hungry brood?
Vain thought! the confines of his throne to trace,
Who glows through all the fields of boundless space.

---

## SONNET TO CAPEL LOFFT, ESQ.

LOFFT, unto thee one tributary song
The simple Muse, admiring, fain would bring;
She longs to lisp thee to the listening throng,
And with thy name to bid the woodlands ring.
Fain would she blazon all thy virtues forth,
Thy warm philanthropy, thy justice mild,
Would say how thou didst foster kindred worth,
And to thy bosom snatch'd Misfortune's child:
Firm she would paint thee, with becoming zeal,
Upright, and learned, as the Pylian sire,
Would say how sweetly thou couldst sweep the lyre,
And show thy labours for the public weal,
Ten thousand virtues tell with joys supreme,
But ah! she shrinks abash'd before the arduous theme.

## SONNET TO THE MOON.

### WRITTEN IN NOVEMBER.

SUBLIME, emerging from the misty verge
Of the horizon dim, thee, Moon, I hail,
As, sweeping o'er the leafless grove, the gale
Seems to repeat the year's funereal dirge.
Now Autumn sickens on the languid sight,
And leaves bestrew the wanderer's lonely way,
Now unto thee, pale arbitress of night,
With double joy my homage do I pay.
When clouds disguise the glories of the day,
And stern November sheds her boisterous blight,
How doubly sweet to mark the moony ray
Shoot through the mist from the ethereal height,
And, still unchanged, back to the memory bring
The smiles Favonian of life's earliest spring.

---

## SONNET WRITTEN AT THE GRAVE OF A FRIEND.

FAST from the west the fading day-streaks fly,
And ebon Night assumes her solemn sway,
Yet here alone, unheeding time, I lie,
And o'er my friend still pour the plaintive lay.
Oh! 'tis not long since, George, with thee I woo'd
The maid of musings by yon moaning wave;

And hail'd the moon's mild beam, which, now re-
new'd,
Seems sweetly sleeping on thy silent grave!
The busy world pursues its boisterous way,
The noise of revelry still echoes round,
Yet I am sad while all beside is gay;
Yet still I weep o'er thy deserted mound.
Oh! that, like thee, I might bid sorrow cease,
And 'neath the greensward sleep the sleep of peace.

---

## SONNET TO MISFORTUNE.

MISFORTUNE, I am young, my chin is bare,
And I have wonder'd much when men have told,
How youth was free from sorrow and from care,
That thou shouldst dwell with me, and leave the
old.
Sure dost not like me! — Shrivel'd hag of hate,
My phiz, and thanks to thee, is sadly long;
I am not either, beldame, over strong;
Nor do I wish at all to be thy mate,
For thou, sweet Fury, art my utter hate.
Nay, shake not thus thy miserable pate;
I am yet young, and do not like thy face;
And, lest thou shouldst resume the wild-goose chase,
I'll tell thee something all thy heat to assuage,
— Thou wilt not hit my fancy in my age.

## SONNET.

As thus oppress'd with many a heavy care
  (Though young yet sorrowful), I turn my feet
  To the dark woodland, longing much to greet
The form of Peace, if chance she sojourn there;
Deep thought and dismal, verging to despair,
  Fills my sad breast; and, tired with this vain coil,
  I shrink dismay'd before life's upland toil.
And as, amid the leaves, the evening air
Whispers still melody, — I think ere long,
  When I no more can hear, these woods will speak;
  And then a sad smile plays upon my cheek,
And mournful phantasies upon me throng,
And I do ponder, with most strange delight,
On the calm slumbers of the dead man's night.

---

## SONNET TO APRIL.

Emblem of life! see changeful April sail
  In varying vest along the shadowy skies,
  Now bidding summer's softest zephyrs rise,
Anon recalling winter's stormy gale,
And pouring from the cloud her sudden hail;
  Then, smiling through the tear that dims her eyes,
  While Iris with her braid the welkin dyes,
Promise of sunshine, not so prone to fail.

So, to us, sojourners in life's low vale,
  The smiles of fortune flatter to deceive,
  While still the fates the web of misery weave.
So Hope exultant spreads her aëry sail,
And from the present gloom the soul conveys
To distant summers and far happier days.

---

## SONNET.

Ye unseen spirits, whose wild melodies,
  At evening rising slow, yet sweetly clear,
  Steal on the musing poet's pensive ear,
As by the wood-spring stretch'd supine he lies;
When he, who now invokes you, low is laid,
  His tired frame resting on the earth's cold bed;
Hold ye your nightly vigils o'er his head,
  And chant a dirge to his reposing shade!
For he was wont to love your madrigals;
  And often by the haunted stream, that laves
  The dark sequester'd woodland's inmost caves,
Would sit and listen to the dying falls,
Till the full tear would quiver in his eye,
And his big heart would heave with mournful
    ecstasy.

## SONNET TO A TAPER.

'Tis midnight. On the globe dead slumber sits,
  And all is silence — in the hour of sleep;
Save when the hollow gust, that swells by fits,
  In the dark wood roars fearfully and deep.
I wake alone to listen and to weep,
  To watch my taper, thy pale beacon burn;
And, as still Memory does her vigils keep,
  To think of days that never can return.
By thy pale ray I raise my languid head,
  My eye surveys the solitary gloom;
And the sad meaning tear, unmix'd with dread,
  Tells thou dost light me to the silent tomb.
Like thee I wane; — like thine my life's last ray
Will fade in loneliness, unwept, away.

---

## SONNET TO MY MOTHER.

And canst thou, Mother, for a moment think
  That we, thy children, when old age shall shed
  Its blanching honours on thy weary head,
Could from our best of duties ever shrink?
Sooner the sun from his high sphere should sink
  Than we, ungrateful, leave thee in that day,
  To pine in solitude thy life away,
Or shun thee, tottering on the grave's cold brink.

Banish the thought! — where'er our steps may roam,
  O'er smiling plains, or wastes without a tree,
  Still will fond memory point our hearts to thee,
And paint the pleasures of thy peaceful home;
While duty bids us all thy griefs assuage,
And smooth the pillow of thy sinking age.

## SONNET.

Yes, 'twill be over soon. — This sickly dream
  Of life will vanish from my feverish brain;
And death my wearied spirit will redeem
  From this wild region of unvaried pain.
Yon brook will glide as softly as before,
  Yon landscape smile, yon golden harvest grow,
Yon sprightly lark on mountain wing will soar
  When Henry's name is heard no more below.
I sigh when all my youthful friends caress,
  They laugh in health, and future evils brave;
Them shall a wife and smiling children bless,
  While I am mouldering in the silent grave.
God of the just, Thou gavest the bitter cup;
I bow to thy behest, and drink it up.

## SONNET TO CONSUMPTION.

Gently, most gently, on thy victim's head,
  Consumption, lay thine hand! — let me decay
  Like the expiring lamp, unseen, away,
And softly go to slumber with the dead.

And if 'tis true what holy men have said,
That strains angelic oft foretell the day
Of death to those good men who fall thy prey,
O let the aërial music round my bed,
Dissolving sad in dying symphony,
Whisper the solemn warning in mine ear;
That I may bid my weeping friends good-by
Ere I depart upon my journey drear:
And, smiling faintly on the painful past,
Compose my decent head, and breathe my last.

---

## SONNET.

TRANSLATED FROM THE FRENCH OF M. DESBARREAUX.

Thy judgments, Lord, are just; thou lovest to wear
The face of pity and of love divine;
But mine is guilt — thou must not, canst not spare,
While heaven is true, and equity is thine.
Yes, oh my God! — such crimes as mine, so dread,
Leave but the choice of punishment to thee;
Thy interest calls for judgment on my head,
And even thy mercy dares not plead for me!
Thy will be done, since 'tis thy glory's due,
Did from mine eyes the endless torrents flow;
Smite — it is time — though endless death ensue,
I bless the avenging hand that lays me low.
But on what spot shall fall thine anger's flood,
That has not first been drench'd in Christ's atoning blood?

## SONNET.

When I sit musing on the chequer'd past
(A term much darken'd with untimely woes),
My thoughts revert to her, for whom still flows
The tear, though half disown'd; and binding fast
Pride's stubborn cheat to my too yielding heart,
I say to her she robb'd me of my rest,
When that was all my wealth. 'T is true my breast
Received from her this wearying, lingering smart;
Yet, ah! I cannot bid her form depart;
Though wrong'd, I love her — yet in anger love,
For she was most unworthy. — Then I prove
Vindictive joy; and on my stern front gleams,
Throned in dark clouds, inflexible . . .
The native pride of my much injured heart.

## SONNET.

Sweet to the gay of heart is Summer's smile,
Sweet the wild music of the laughing Spring;
But ah! my soul far other scenes beguile,
Where gloomy storms their sullen shadows fling.
Is it for me to strike the Idalian string —
Raise the soft music of the warbling wire,
While in my ears the howls of furies ring,
And melancholy waste the vital fire?

Away with thoughts like these — To some lone cave
Where howls the shrill blast, and where sweeps
the wave,
Direct my steps; there, in the lonely drear,
I'll sit remote from worldly noise, and muse
Till through my soul shall Peace her balm infuse,
And whisper sounds of comfort in mine ear.

## SONNET.

Quick o'er the wintry waste dart fiery shafts —
Bleak blows the blast — now howls — then faintly
dies —
And oft upon its awful wings it wafts
The dying wanderer's distant, feeble cries.
Now, when athwart the gloom gaunt Horror stalks,
And midnight hags their damned vigils hold,
The pensive poet 'mid the wild waste walks,
And ponders on the ills life's paths unfold.
Mindless of dangers hovering round, he goes,
Insensible to every outward ill;
Yet oft his bosom heaves with rending throes,
And oft big tears adown his worn cheeks trill.
Ah! 'tis the anguish of a mental sore,
Which gnaws his heart, and bids him hope no more.

# BALLADS, SONGS, AND HYMNS.

## GONDOLINE.

### A BALLAD.

THE night it was still, and the moon it shone
Serenely on the sea,
And the waves at the foot of the rifted rock
They murmur'd pleasantly,

When Gondoline roam'd along the shore,
A maiden full fair to the sight;
Though love had made bleak the rose on her cheek,
And turn'd it to deadly white.

Her thoughts they were drear, and the silent tear
It fill'd her faint blue eye,
As oft she heard, in fancy's ear,
Her Bertrand's dying sigh.

Her Bertrand was the bravest youth
Of all our good king's men,
And he was gone to the Holy Land
To fight the Saracen.

And many a month had pass'd away,
 And many a rolling year,
But nothing the maid from Palestine
 Could of her lover hear.

Full oft she vainly tried to pierce
 The ocean's misty face;
Full oft she thought her lover's bark
 She on the wave could trace.

And every night she placed a light
 In the high rock's lonely tower,
To guide her lover to the land,
 Should the murky tempest lower.

But now despair had seized her breast,
 And sunken in her eye;
"Oh tell me but if Bertrand live,
 And I in peace will die."

She wander'd o'er the lonely shore,
 The curlew scream'd above,
She heard the scream with a sickening heart,
 Much boding on her love.

Yet still she kept her lonely way,
 And this was all her cry.
"Oh! tell me but if Bertrand live,
 And I in peace shall die."

And now she came to a horrible rift
All in the rock's hard side,
A bleak and blasted oak o'erspread
The cavern yawning wide.

And pendant from its dismal top
The deadly nightshade hung;
The hemlock and the aconite
Across the mouth was flung.

And all within was dark and drear,
And all without was calm;
Yet Gondoline enter'd, her soul upheld
By some deep-working charm.

And as she enter'd the cavern wide,
The moonbeam gleamed pale,
And she saw a snake on the craggy rock,
It clung by its slimy tail.

Her foot it slipp'd, and she stood aghast,
She trod on a bloated toad;
Yet, still upheld by the secret charm,
She kept upon her road.

And now upon her frozen ear
Mysterious sounds arose;
So, on the mountain's piny top
The blustering north wind blows.

Then furious peals of laughter loud
   Were heard with thundering sound,
Till they died away in soft decay,
   Low whispering o'er the ground.

Yet still the maiden onward went,
   The charm yet onward led,
Though each big glaring ball of sight
   Seem'd bursting from her head.

But now a pale blue light she saw,
   It from a distance came;
She follow'd, till upon her sight
   Burst full a flood of flame.

She stood appall'd; yet still the charm
   Upheld her sinking soul;
Yet each bent knee the other smote,
   And each wild eye did roll.

And such a sight as she saw there
   No mortal saw before,
And such a sight as she saw there
   No mortal shall see more.

A burning cauldron stood in the midst,
   The flame was fierce and high,
And all the cave so wide and long
   Was plainly seen thereby.

And round about the cauldron stout
    Twelve wither'd witches stood;
Their waists were bound with living snakes,
    And their hair was stiff with blood.

Their hands were gory too; and red
    And fiercely flamed their eyes:
And they were muttering indistinct
    Their hellish mysteries.

And suddenly they join'd their hands,
    And utter'd a joyous cry,
And round about the cauldron stout
    They danced right merrily.

And now they stopp'd; and each prepared
    To tell what she had done,
Since last the lady of the night
    Her waning course had run.

Behind a rock stood Gondoline,
    Thick weeds her face did veil,
And she lean'd fearful forwarder,
    To hear the dreadful tale.

The first arose: She said she'd seen
    Rare sport since the blind cat mew'd,
She'd been to sea in a leaky sieve,
    And a jovial storm had brew'd.

She'd called around the winged winds,
    And raised a devilish rout;
And she laugh'd so loud, the peals were heard
    Full fifteen leagues about.

She said there was a little bark
    Upon the roaring wave,
And there was a woman there who'd been
    To see her husband's grave.

And she had got a child in her arms,
    It was her only child,
And oft its little infant pranks
    Her heavy heart beguiled.

And there was too in that same bark
    A father and his son:
The lad was sickly, and the sire
    Was old and woe-begone.

And when the tempest waxed strong,
    And the bark could no more it 'bide,
She said it was jovial fun to hear
    How the poor devils cried.

The mother clasp'd her orphan child
    Unto her breast and wept;
And sweetly folded in her arms
    The careless baby slept.

And she told how, in the shape of the wind,
As manfully it roar'd,
She twisted her hand in the infant's hair,
And threw it overboard.

And to have seen the mother's pangs,
'Twas a glorious sight to see;
The crew could scarcely hold her down
From jumping in the sea.

The hag held a lock of her hair in her hand,
And it was soft and fair:
It must have been a lovely child,
To have had such lovely hair.

And she said the father in his arms
He held his sickly son,
And his dying throes they fast arose,
His pains were nearly done.

And she throttled the youth with her sinewy hands,
And his face grew deadly blue;
And the father he tore his thin gray hair,
And kiss'd the livid hue.

And then she told how she bored a hole
In the bark, and it fill'd away:
And 'twas rare to hear how some did swear,
And some did vow and pray.

The man and woman they soon were dead,
    The sailors their strength did urge;
But the billows that beat were their winding-sheet,
    And the winds sung their funeral dirge.

She threw the infant's hair in the fire,
    The red flame flamed high,
And round about the cauldron stout
    They danced right merrily.

The second begun: She said she had done
    The task that Queen Hecate had set her,
And that the devil, the father of evil,
    Had never accomplish'd a better.

She said, there was an aged woman,
    And she had a daughter fair,
Whose evil habits fill'd her heart
    With misery and care.

The daughter had a paramour,
    A wicked man was he,
And oft the woman him against
    Did murmur grievously.

And the hag had work'd the daughter up
    To murder her old mother,
That then she might seize on all her goods,
    And wanton with her lover.

And one night as the old woman
  Was sick and ill in bed,
And pondering solely on the life
  Her wicked daughter led,

She heard her footstep on the floor,
  And she raised her pallid head,
And she saw her daughter, with a knife,
  Approaching to her bed.

And said, My child, I'm very ill,
  I have not long to live,
Now kiss my cheek, that ere I die
  Thy sins I may forgive.

And the murderess bent to kiss her cheek,
  And she lifted the sharp bright knife,
And the mother saw her fell intent,
  And hard she begg'd for life.

But prayers would nothing her avail,
  And she scream'd aloud with fear,
But the house was lone, and the piercing screams
  Could reach no human ear.

And though that she was sick, and old,
  She struggled hard, and fought;
The murderess cut three fingers through
  Ere she could reach her throat.

And the hag she held her fingers up,
The skin was mangled sore,
And they all agreed a nobler deed
Was never done before.

And she threw the fingers in the fire,
The red flame flamed high,
And round about the cauldron stout
They danced right merrily.

The third arose: She said she'd been
To holy Palestine;
And seen more blood in one short day
Than they had all seen in nine.

Now Gondoline, with fearful steps,
Drew nearer to the flame,
For much she dreaded now to hear
Her hapless lover's name.

The hag related then the sports
Of that eventful day,
When on the well contested field
Full fifteen thousand lay.

She said that she in human gore
Above the knees did wade,
And that no tongue could truly tell
The tricks she there had play'd.

There was a gallant featured youth,
    Who like a hero fought;
He kiss'd a bracelet on his wrist,
    And every danger sought.

And in a vassal's garb disguised,
    Unto the knight she sues,
And tells him she from Britain comes,
    And brings unwelcome news.

That three days ere she had embark'd
    His love had given her hand
Unto a wealthy Thane: — and thought
    Him dead in Holy Land.

And to have seen how he did writhe
    When this her tale she told,
It would have made a wizard's blood
    Within his heart run cold.

Then fierce he spurr'd his warrior steed,
    And sought the battle's bed;
And soon all mangled o'er with wounds
    He on the cold turf bled.

And from his smoking corse she tore
    His head, half clove in two.
She ceased, and from beneath her garb
    The bloody trophy drew.

The eyes were starting from their socks,
    The mouth it ghastly grinn'd,
And there was a gash across the brow,
    The scalp was nearly skinn'd.

'T was Bertrand's head! With a terrible scream
    The maiden gave a spring
And from her fearful hiding-place
    She fell into the ring.

The lights they fled — the cauldron sunk,
    Deep thunders shook the dome,
And hollow peals of laughter came
    Resounding through the gloom.

Insensible the maiden lay
    Upon the hellish ground,
And still mysterious sounds were heard
    At intervals around.

She woke — she half arose — and wild
    She cast a horrid glare,
The sounds had ceased, the lights had fled,
    And all was stillness there.

And through an awning in the rock
    The moon it sweetly shone,
And show'd a river in the cave
    Which dismally did moan.

The stream was black, it sounded deep
As it rush'd the rocks between,
It offer'd well, for madness fired
The breast of Gondoline.

She plunged in, the torrent moan'd
With its accustom'd sound,
And hollow peals of laughter loud
Again rebellow'd round.

The maid was seen no more. — But oft
Her ghost is known to glide,
At midnight's silent, solemn hour,
Along the ocean's side.

---

## A BALLAD.

Be hush'd, be hush'd, ye bitter winds,
Ye pelting rains, a little rest;
Lie still, lie still, ye busy thoughts,
That wring with grief my aching breast.

Oh! cruel was my faithless love,
To triumph o'er an artless maid;
Oh! cruel was my faithless love,
To leave the breast by him betray'd.

When exiled from my native home,
He should have wiped the bitter tear;
Nor left me faint and lone to roam,
A heart-sick weary wanderer here.

My child moans sadly in my arms,
The winds they will not let it sleep:
Ah, little knows the hapless babe
What makes its wretched mother weep!

Now lie thee still, my infant dear,
I cannot bear thy sobs to see,
Harsh is thy father, little one,
And never will he shelter thee.

Oh, that I were but in my grave,
And winds were piping o'er me loud,
And thou, my poor, my orphan babe,
Wert nestling in thy mother's shroud!

## THE LULLABY OF A FEMALE CONVICT TO HER CHILD THE NIGHT PREVIOUS TO EXECUTION.

Sleep, baby mine,* enkerchieft on my bosom,
Thy cries they pierce again my bleeding breast;
Sleep, baby mine, not long thou 'lt have a mother
To lull thee fondly in her arms to rest.

Baby, why dost thou keep this sad complaining?
Long from mine eyes have kindly slumbers fled;
Hush, hush, my babe, the night is quickly waning,
And I would fain compose my aching head.

* Sir Philip Sidney has a poem, beginning, "Sleep, baby mine."

Poor wayward wretch! and who will heed thy weeping,
When soon an outcast on the world thou'lt be?
Who then will soothe thee, when thy mother's sleeping
In her low grave of shame and infamy?

Sleep, baby mine — To-morrow I must leave thee,
And I would snatch an interval of rest:
Sleep these last moments ere the laws bereave thee,
For never more thou'lt press a mother's breast.

---

## THE SAVOYARD'S RETURN.

Oh! yonder is the well known spot,
My dear, my long lost native home!
Oh, welcome is yon little cot,
Where I shall rest, no more to roam!
Oh! I have travell'd far and wide,
O'er many a distant foreign land;
Each place, each province I have tried,
And sung and danced my saraband.
But all their charms could not prevail
To steal my heart from yonder vale.

Of distant climes the false report
It lured me from my native land;

It bade me rove — my sole support
  My cymbals and my saraband.
The woody dell, the hanging rock,
  The chamois skipping o'er the heights;
The plain adorn'd with many a flock,
  And, oh! a thousand more delights,
    That grace yon dear beloved retreat,
    Have backward won my weary feet.

Now safe return'd, with wandering tired,
  No more my little home I'll leave;
And many a tale of what I've seen
  Shall while away the winter's eve.
Oh! I have wandered far and wide,
  O'er many a distant foreign land;
Each place, each province I have tried,
  And sung and danced my saraband;
    But all their charms could not prevail
    To steal my heart from yonder vale.

## A PASTORAL SONG.

Come, Anna! come, the morning dawns,
  Faint streaks of radiance tinge the skies;
Come, let us seek the dewy lawns,
  And watch the early lark arise;
    While nature, clad in vesture gay,
    Hails the loved return of day.

Our flocks, that nip the scanty blade
  Upon the moor, shall seek the vale;
And then, secure beneath the shade,
  We'll listen to the throstle's tale;
    And watch the silver clouds above,
    As o'er the azure vault they rove.

Come, Anna! come, and bring thy lute,
  That with its tones, so softly sweet,
In cadence with my mellow flute,
  We may beguile the noontide heat;
    While near the mellow bee shall join,
    To raise a harmony divine.

And then at eve, when silence reigns,
  Except when heard the beetle's hum,
We'll leave the sober tinted plains,
  To these sweet heights again we'll come;
    And thou to thy soft lute shalt play
    A solemn vesper to departing day.

---

## MELODY.

Yes, once more that dying strain,
  Anna, touch thy lute for me;
Sweet, when pity's tones complain,
  Doubly sweet is melody.

While the Virtues thus enweave
  Mildly soft the thrilling song,
Winter's long and lonesome eve
  Glides unfelt, unseen, along.

Thus when life hath stolen away,
  And the wintry night is near,
Thus shall virtue's friendly ray
  Age's closing evening, cheer.

---

## SONG.

### BY WALLER.

A Lady of Cambridge lent Waller's Poems to the Author, and when he returned them to her, she discovered an additional stanza written by him at the bottom of the song here copied.

    Go, lovely rose!
Tell her, that wastes her time on me,
    That now she knows,
When I resemble her to thee,
How sweet and fair she seems to be.

    Tell her that's young,
And shuns to have her graces spied,
    That hadst thou sprung
In deserts, where no men abide,
Thou must have uncommended died.

Small is the worth
Of beauty from the light retired,
Bid her come forth,
Suffer herself to be desired,
And not blush so to be admired.

Then die, that she
The common fate of all things rare
May read in thee;
How small a part of time they share,
That are so wondrous sweet and fair.

[Yet, though thou fade,
From thy dead leaves let fragrance rise;
And teach the maid
That Goodness Time's rude hand defies,
That Virtue lives when Beauty dies.
H. K. WHITE.]

---

## THE WANDERING BOY.

### A SONG.

When the winter wind whistles along the wild moor,
And the cottager shuts on the beggar his door;
When the chilling tear stands in my comfortless eye,
Oh, how hard is the lot of the Wandering Boy.

The winter is cold, and I have no vest,
And my heart it is cold as it beats in my breast;
No father, no mother, no kindred have I,
For I am a parentless Wandering Boy.

Yet I had a home, and I once had a sire,
A mother who granted each infant desire;
Our cottage it stood in a wood-embower'd vale,
Where the ringdove would warble its sorrowful
tale.

But my father and mother were summon'd away,
And they left me to hard-hearted strangers a prey;
I fled from their rigour with many a sigh,
And now I'm a poor little Wandering Boy.

The wind it is keen, and the snow loads the gale,
And no one will list to my innocent tale;
I'll go to the grave where my parents both lie,
And death shall befriend the poor Wandering Boy.

## CANZONET.

Maiden! wrap thy mantle round thee,
Cold the rain beats on thy breast:
Why should Horror's voice astound thee?
Death can bid the wretched rest!

All under the tree
Thy bed may be,
And thou mayst slumber peacefully.

Maiden! once gay pleasure knew thee,
Now thy cheeks are pale and deep:
Love has been a felon to thee,
Yet, poor maiden, do not weep:
There's rest for thee
All under the tree,
Where thou wilt sleep most peacefully.

---

## SONG.

WRITTEN AT THE AGE OF FOURTEEN.

Softly, softly blow, ye breezes,
Gently o'er my Edwy fly!
Lo! he slumbers, slumbers sweetly;
Softly, zephyrs, pass him by!
My love is asleep,
He lies by the deep,
All along where the salt waves sigh.

I have cover'd him with rushes,
Water-flags, and branches dry.
Edwy, long have been thy slumbers;
Edwy, Edwy, ope thine eye!

My love is asleep,
He lies by the deep,
All along where the salt waves sigh.

Still he sleeps; he will not waken,
Fastly closed is his eye;
Paler is his cheek, and chiller
Than the icy moon on high.
Alas! he is dead,
He has chose his death-bed
All along where the salt waves sigh.

Is it, is it so, my Edwy?
Will thy slumbers never fly?
Couldst thou think I would survive thee?
No, my love, thou bid'st me die.
Thou bid'st me seek
Thy death-bed bleak
All along where the salt waves sigh.

I will gently kiss thy cold lips,
On thy breast I'll lay my head,
And the winds shall sing our death dirge,
And our shroud the waters spread;
The moon will smile sweet,
And the wild wave will beat,
Oh! so softly o'er our lonely bed.

## THE SHIPWRECKED SOLITARY'S SONG TO THE NIGHT.

Thou, spirit of the spangled night!
I woo thee from the watchtower high,
Where thou dost sit to guide the bark
Of lonely mariner.

The winds are whistling o'er the wolds,
The distant main is moaning low;
Come, let us sit and weave a song—
A melancholy song!

Sweet is the scented gale of morn,
And sweet the noontide's fervid beam,
But sweeter far the solemn calm
That marks thy mournful reign.

I've pass'd here many a lonely year,
And never human voice have heard;
I've pass'd here many a lonely year,
A solitary man.

And I have linger'd in the shade,
From sultry noon's hot beams; and I
Have knelt before my wicker door,
To sing my evening song.

And I have hail'd the gray morn high,
On the blue mountain's misty brow,
And tried to tune my little reed
To hymns of harmony.

But never could I tune my reed,
At morn, or noon, or eve, so sweet,
As when upon the ocean shore
I hail'd thy star-beam mild.

The dayspring brings not joy to me,
The moon it whispers not of peace;
But oh! when darkness robes the heavens,
My woes are mix'd with joy.

And then I talk, and often think
Aërial voices answer me;
And oh! I am not then alone—
A solitary man.

And when the blustering winter winds
Howl in the woods that clothe my cave,
I lay me on my lonely mat,
And pleasant are my dreams.

And fancy gives me back my wife;
And fancy gives me back my child;
She gives me back my little home,
And all its placid joys.

Then hateful is the morning hour,
That calls me from the dream of bliss,
To find myself still lone, and hear
The same dull sounds again.

The deep-toned winds, the moaning sea,
The whispering of the boding trees,
The brook's eternal flow, and oft
The condor's hollow scream.

---

## THE WONDERFUL JUGGLER.

### A SONG.

Come all ye true hearts, who, Old England to save,
Now shoulder the musket, or plough the rough wave,
I will sing you a song of a wonderful fellow,
Who has ruin'd Jack Pudding, and broke Punchinello.
Derry down, down, high derry down.

This juggler is little, and ugly, and black,
But, like Atlas, he stalks with the world at his back;
'Tis certain, all fear of the devil he scorns;
Some say they are cousins; we know he wears horns.
Derry down.

At hop, skip, and jump, who so famous as he?
He hopp'd o'er an army, he skipp'd o'er the sea;
And he jump'd from the desk of a village attorney
To the throne of the Bourbons — a pretty long journey.
Derry down.

He tosses up kingdoms the same as a ball,
And his cup is so fashion'd it catches them all;
The Pope and Grand Turk have been heard to declare
His skill at the long bow has made them both stare.
Derry down.

He has shown off his tricks in France, Italy, Spain;
And Germany too knows his legerdemain;
So hearing John Bull has a taste for strange sights,
He's coming to London to put us to rights.
Derry down.

To encourage his puppets to venture this trip,
He has built them such boats as can conquer a ship;
With a gun of good metal, that shoots out so far,
It can silence the broadsides of three men of war.
Derry down.

This new Katterfelto, his show to complete,
Means his boats should all sink as they pass by our fleet;

Then, as under the ocean their course they steer
right on, [Triton.
They can pepper their foes from the bed of old
Derry down.

If this project should fail, he has others in store;
Wooden horses, for instance, may bring them safe
o'er;
Or the genius of France (as the Moniteur tells)
May order balloons, or provide diving-bells.
Derry down.

When Philip of Spain fitted out his Armada,
Britain saw his designs, and could meet her invader;
But how to greet Bonny she never will know,
If he comes in the style of a fish or a crow.
Derry down.

Now if our rude tars will so crowd up the seas,
That his boats have not room to go down when they
please,
Can't he wait till the channel is quite frozen over,
And a stout pair of skates will transport him to
Dover. Derry down.

How welcome he'll be it were needless to say;
Neither he nor his puppets shall e'er go away;
I am sure at his heels we shall constantly stick,
Till we know he has play'd off his very last trick.
Derry down, down, high derry down.

## HYMN.

In Heaven we shall be purified, so as to be able to endure the splendours of the Deity.

AWAKE, sweet harp of Judah, wake,
Retune thy strings for Jesus' sake;
We sing the Saviour of our race,
The Lamb, our shield, and hiding-place.

When God's right arm is bared for war,
And thunders clothe his cloudy car,
Where, where, oh, where shall man retire,
To escape the horrors of his ire?

'Tis he, the Lamb, to him we fly,
While the dread tempest passes by;
God sees his Well-beloved's face,
And spares us in our hiding-place.

Thus while we dwell in this low scene,
The Lamb is our unfailing screen;
To him, though guilty, still we run,
And God still spares us for his Son.

While yet we sojourn here below,
Pollutions still our hearts o'erflow;
Fallen, abject, mean, a sentenced race,
We deeply need a hiding-place.

Yet, courage — days and years will glide,
And we shall lay these clods aside,
Shall be baptized in Jordan's flood,
And wash'd in Jesus' cleansing blood.

Then pure, immortal, sinless, freed,
We through the Lamb shall be decreed;
Shall meet the Father face to face,
And need no more a hiding-place.*

## A HYMN FOR FAMILY WORSHIP.

O Lord, another day is flown,
    And we, a lonely band,
Are met once more before thy throne,
    To bless thy fostering hand.

And wilt thou bend a listening ear,
    To praises low as ours?
Thou wilt! for thou dost love to hear
    The song which meekness pours.

And, Jesus, thou thy smiles wilt deign,
    As we before thee pray;
For thou didst bless the infant train,
    And we are less than they.

* The last stanza of this hymn was added extemporaneously, by the Author, one summer evening, when he was with a few friends on the Trent, and singing as he was used to do on such occasions.

O let thy grace perform its part,
And let contention cease;
And shed abroad in every heart
Thine everlasting peace!

Thus chasten'd, cleansed, entirely thine,
A flock by Jesus led;
The Sun of Holiness shall shine
In glory on our head.

And thou wilt turn our wandering feet,
And thou wilt bless our way;
Till worlds shall fade, and faith shall greet
The dawn of lasting day.

---

## THE STAR OF BETHLEHEM.

When marshal'd on the nightly plain,
The glittering host bestud the sky;
One star alone, of all the train,
Can fix the sinner's wandering eye.

Hark! hark! to God the chorus breaks,
From every host, from every gem;
But one alone the Saviour speaks,
It is the Star of Bethlehem.

Once on the raging seas I rode,
The storm was loud,—the night was dark,
The ocean yawn'd—and rudely blow'd
The wind that toss'd my foundering bark.

Deep horror then my vitals froze,
    Death-struck, I ceased the tide to stem;
When suddenly a star arose,
    It was the Star of Bethlehem.

It was my guide, my light, my all,
    It bade my dark forebodings cease;
And through the storm and dangers' thrall
    It led me to the port of peace.

Now safely moor'd — my peril's o'er,
    I'll sing, first in night's diadem,
For ever, and for evermore,
    The Star! — The Star of Bethlehem!

---

## A HYMN.

O Lord, my God, in mercy turn,
In mercy hear a sinner mourn!
To thee I call, to thee I cry,
O leave me, leave me not to die!

I strove against thee, Lord, I know,
I spurn'd thy grace, I mock'd thy law;
The hour is past — the day's gone by,
And I am left alone to die.

O pleasures past, what are ye now
But thorns about my bleeding brow!
Spectres that hover round my brain,
And aggravate and mock my pain.

For pleasure I have given my soul;
Now, Justice, let thy thunders roll!
Now, Vengeance, smile — and with a blow
Lay the rebellious ingrate low.

Yet, Jesus, Jesus! there I'll cling,
I'll crowd beneath his sheltering wing;
I'll clasp the cross, and holding there,
Even me, oh bliss! — his wrath may spare.

# TRIBUTARY VERSES.

## EULOGY ON HENRY KIRKE WHITE, BY LORD BYRON.

FROM THE ENGLISH BARDS AND SCOTCH REVIEWERS.

UNHAPPY White!* while life was in its spring,
And thy young muse just waved her joyous wing,
The spoiler came; and all thy promise fair
Has sought the grave, to sleep for ever there.
Oh! what a noble heart was here undone,
When science self destroy'd her favourite son!
Yes! she too much indulged thy fond pursuit,
She sow'd the seeds, but death has reap'd the fruit.
'Twas thine own genius gave the final blow,
And help'd to plant the wound that laid thee low.
So the struck eagle, stretch'd upon the plain,

* Henry Kirke White died at Cambridge in October, 1806, in consequence of too much exertion in the pursuit of studies that would have matured a mind which disease and poverty could not impair, and which death itself destroyed rather than subdued. His poems abound in such beauties as must impress the reader with the liveliest regret that so short a period was allotted to talents, which would have dignified even the sacred functions he was destined to assume.

No more through rolling clouds to soar again,
View'd his own feather on the fatal dart,
And wing'd the shaft that quiver'd in his heart.
Keen were his pangs, but keener far to feel,
He nursed the pinion which impell'd the steel;
While the same plumage that had warm'd his nest
Drank the last life-drop of his bleeding breast.

---

## SONNET ON HENRY KIRKE WHITE.

BY CAPEL LOFFT.

Master so early of the various lyre
  Energic, pure, sublime! — Thus art thou gone?
  In its bright dawn of fame that spirit flown,
Which breathed such sweetness, tenderness, and fire!
Wert thou but shown to win us to admire,
  And veil in death thy splendour? — But unknown
  Their destination who least time have shone,
And brightest beam'd. —When these the Eternal Sire,
— Righteous, and wise, and good are all his ways —
  Eclipses as their sun begins to rise,
Can mortal judge, for their diminish'd days,
  What blest equivalent in changeless skies,
What sacred glory waits them? — His the praise;
  Gracious, whate'er he gives, whate'er denies.

24th Oct. 1806.

## SONNET OCCASIONED BY THE SECOND OF HENRY KIRKE WHITE.

BY CAPEL LOFFT.

YES, fled already is thy vital fire,
And the fair promise of thy early bloom
Lost, in youth's morn extinct; sunk in the tomb;
Mute in the grave sleeps thy enchanted lyre!
And is it vainly that our souls aspire?
Falsely does the presaging heart presume
That we shall live beyond life's cares and gloom;
Grasps it eternity with high desire,
But to imagine bliss, feel woe, and die;
Leaving survivors to worse pangs than death?
Not such the sanction of the Eternal Mind.
The harmonious order of the starry sky,
And awful revelation's angel breath,
Assure these hopes their full effect shall find.

25th December, 1806.

## WRITTEN IN THE HOMER OF MR. H. K. WHITE.

PRESENTED TO ME BY HIS BROTHER, J. NEVILLE WHITE.

BY CAPEL LOFFT.

BARD of brief days, but ah, of deathless fame!
While on these awful leaves my fond eyes rest,
On which thine late have dwelt, thy hand late press'd,
I pause; and gaze regretful on thy name.
By neither chance nor envy, time nor flame,
Be it from this its mansion dispossess'd!
But thee, Eternity, clasps to her breast,
And in celestial splendour thrones thy claim.

No more with mortal pencil shalt thou trace
An imitative radiance: * thy pure lyre
Springs from our changeful atmosphere's embrace,
And beams and breathes in empyreal fire:
The Homeric and Miltonian sacred tone
Responsive hail that lyre congenial to their own.

Bury, 11th Jan. 1807.

* Alluding to his pencilled sketch of a head surrounded with a glory.

## TO THE MEMORY OF H. K. WHITE.

BY THE REV. W. B. COLLYER, A. M.

O LOST too soon! accept the tear
A stranger to thy memory pays!
Dear to the muse, to science dear,
In the young morning of thy days!

All the wild notes that pity loved
Awoke, responsive still to thee,
While o'er the lyre thy fingers roved
In softest, sweetest harmony.

The chords that in the human heart
Compassion touches as her own,
Bore in thy symphonies a part—
With them in perfect unison.

Amidst accumulated woes
That premature afflictions bring,
Submission's sacred hymn arose,
Warbled from every mournful string.

When o'er thy dawn the darkness spread,
And deeper every moment grew;
When rudely round thy youthful head
The chilling blasts of sickness blew;

Religion heard no 'plainings loud,
  The sigh in secret stole from thee;
And pity, from the "dropping cloud,"
  Shed tears of holy sympathy.

Cold is that heart in which were met
  More virtues than could ever die;
The morning star of hope is set—
  The sun adorns another sky.

O partial grief! to mourn the day
  So suddenly o'erclouded here,
To rise with unextinguish'd ray—
  To shine in a superior sphere!

Oft Genius early quits this sod,
  Impatient of a robe of clay,
Spreads the light pinion, spurns the clod,
  And smiles, and soars, and steals away!

But more than genius urged thy flight,
  And mark'd the way, dear youth! for thee:
Henry sprang up to worlds of light
  On wings of immortality!

Blackheath Hill, 24th June, 1808.

## SONNET TO HENRY KIRKE WHITE, ON HIS POEMS LATELY PUBLISHED.

BY ARTHUR OWEN, ESQ.

HAIL! gifted youth, whose passion-breathing lay
  Portrays a mind attuned to noblest themes,
  A mind, which, wrapt in Fancy's high-wrought
      dreams,
To nature's veriest bounds its daring way
Can wing: what charms throughout thy pages shine,
  To win with fairy thrill the melting soul!
  For though along impassion'd grandeur roll,
Yet in full power simplicity is thine.
Proceed, sweet bard! and the heaven-granted fire
  Of pity, glowing in thy feeling breast,
  May nought destroy, may nought thy soul divest
Of joy — of rapture in the living lyre,
  Thou tunest so magically: but may fame
  Each passing year add honours to thy name.

Richmond, Sept. 1803.

## SONNET,

ON SEEING ANOTHER WRITTEN TO H. K. WHITE, IN SEPTEMBER, 1803, INSERTED IN HIS "REMAINS."

BY ARTHUR OWEN, ESQ.

Ah! once again the long left wires among,
Truants the Muse to weave her requiem song;
With sterner lore now busied, erst the lay
Cheer'd my dark morn of manhood, wont to stray
O'er fancy's fields in quest of musky flower;
To me nor fragrant less, though barr'd from view
And courtship of the world: hail'd was the hour
That gave me, dripping fresh with nature's dew,
Poor Henry's budding beauties — to a clime
Hapless transplanted, whose exotic ray
Forced their young vigour into transient day,
And drain'd the stalk that rear'd them! and shall time
Trample these orphan blossoms? — No! they breathe
Still lovelier charms — for Southey culls the wreath!

Oxford, Dec. 17, 1807.

## REFLECTIONS ON READING THE LIFE OF THE LATE HENRY KIRKE WHITE.

BY WILLIAM HOLLOWAY,
AUTHOR OF THE "PEASANT'S FATE."

Darling of science and the muse,
How shall a son of song refuse
  To shed a tear for thee?
To us, so soon, for ever lost,
What hopes, what prospects have been cross'd
  By Heaven's supreme decree?

How could a parent, love-beguiled,
In life's fair prime resign a child
  So duteous, good, and kind?
The warblers of the soothing strain
Must string the elegiac lyre in vain
  To soothe the wounded mind!

Yet, Fancy, hovering round the tomb,
Half envies, while she mourns thy doom,
  Dear poet, saint, and sage!
Who into one short span, at best,
The wisdom of an age compress'd,
  A patriarch's lengthen'd age!

To him a genius sanctified,
And purged from literary pride,
  A sacred boon was given:
Chaste as the psalmist's harp, his lyre
Celestial raptures could inspire,
  And lift the soul to Heaven.

'T was not the laurel earth bestows,
'T was not the praise from man that flows,
  With classic toil he sought:
He sought the crown that martyrs wear,
When rescued from a world of care;
  Their spirit too he caught.

Here come, ye thoughtless, vain, and gay,
Who idly range in Folly's way,
  And learn the worth of time:
Learn ye, whose days have run to waste,
How to redeem this pearl at last,
  Atoning for your crime.

This flower, that droop'd in one cold clime
Transplanted from the soil of time
  To immortality,
In full perfection there shall bloom;
And those who now lament his doom
  Must bow to God's decree.

London, 27th Feb. 1808

## ON THE DEATH OF HENRY KIRKE WHITE.

BY T. PARK.

Too, too prophetic did thy wild note swell,
  Impassion'd minstrel! when its pitying wail
Sigh'd o'er the vernal primrose as it fell
  Untimely, wither'd by the northern gale.*
Thou wert that flower of promise and of prime!
  Whose opening bloom, 'mid many an adverse
      blast, [clime,
Charm'd the lone wanderer through this desert
  But charm'd him with a rapture soon o'ercast,
To see thee languish into quick decay.
  Yet was not thy departing immature;
For ripe in virtue thou wert reft away,
  And pure in spirit, as the bless'd are pure;
Pure as the dewdrop, freed from earthly leaven,
That sparkles, is exhaled, and blends with heaven!

---

## LINES ON THE DEATH OF MR. HENRY KIRKE WHITE.

BY THE REV. J. PLUMPTRE.

Such talents and such piety combined,
With such unfeign'd humility of mind,
Bespoke him fair to tread the way to fame,
And live an honour to the Christian name.

* See Clifton Grove.

But Heaven was pleased to stop his fleeting hour,
And blight the fragrance of the opening flower.
We mourn — but not for him, removed from pain;
Our loss, we trust, is his eternal gain:
With him we'll strive to win the Saviour's love,
And hope to join him with the blest above.

October 24th, 1806.

## TO MR. HENRY KIRKE WHITE.

BY H. WELKER.

HARK! 'tis some sprite who sweeps a funeral knell,
  For Dermody no more. — That fitful tone
From Eolus' wild harp alone can swell,
  Or Chatterton assumes the lyre unknown.

No; list again! 'tis Bateman's fatal sigh
  Swells with the breeze, and dies upon the stream:
'T is Margaret mourns, as swift she rushes by,
  Roused by the demons from adulterous dream.

O! say, sweet youth! what genius fires thy soul?
  The same which tuned the frantic nervous strain
To the wild harp of Collins? — By the pole,
  Or 'mid the seraphim and heavenly train,
Taught Milton everlasting secrets to unfold,
To sing Hell's flaming gulf, or Heaven high arch'd
    with gold?

## VERSES OCCASIONED BY THE DEATH OF HENRY KIRKE WHITE.

BY JOSIAH CONDER.

What is this world at best,
Though deck'd in vernal bloom,
By hope and youthful fancy dress'd,
What, but a ceaseless toil for rest,
A passage to the tomb?
If flowrets strew
The avenue,
Though fair, alas! how fading, and how few!

And every hour comes arm'd
By sorrow, or by woe:
Conceal'd beneath its little wings,
A scythe the soft-shod pilferer brings,
To lay some comfort low:
Some tie to unbind,
By love entwined,
Some silken bond that holds the captive mind.

And every month displays
The ravages of time:
Faded the flowers! — The spring is past!
The scatter'd leaves, the wintry blast,
Warn to a milder clime:

16

The songsters flee
The leafless tree,
And bear to happier realms their melody.

Henry! the world no more
Can claim thee for her own!
In purer skies thy radiance beams!
Thy lyre employ'd on nobler themes
Before the eternal throne:
Yet, spirit dear,
Forgive the tear
Which those must shed who're doom'd to linger here.

Although a stranger, I
In friendship's train would weep:
Lost to the world, alas! so young,
And must thy lyre, in silence hung,
On the dark cypress sleep?
The poet, all
Their friend may call;
And Nature's self attends his funeral.

Although with feeble wing
Thy flight I would pursue,
With quicken'd zeal, with humbled pride,
Alike our object, hopes, and guide,
One heaven alike in view;
True, it was thine
To tower, to shine;
But I may make thy milder virtues mine.

If Jesus own my name
(Though fame pronounced it never),
Sweet spirit, not with thee alone,
But all whose absence here I moan,
Circling with harps the golden throne,
I shall unite for ever.
At death then why
Tremble or sigh? [to die?
Oh! who would wish to live, but he who fears

Dec. 5, 1807.

---

## ON READING HENRY KIRKE WHITE'S POEM ON SOLITUDE.

BY JOSIAH CONDER.

But art thou thus indeed "alone?"
Quite unbefriended — all unknown?
And hast thou then his name forgot
Who form'd thy frame, and fix'd thy lot?

Is not his voice in evening's gale?
Beams not with him the "star" so pale?
Is there a leaf can fade and die
Unnoticed by his watchful eye?

Each fluttering hope — each anxious fear —
Each lonely sigh — each silent tear —
To thine Almighty Friend are known;
And say'st thou, thou art "all alone?"

## ODE ON THE LATE H. KIRKE WHITE.

BY JUVENIS.

AND is the minstrel's voyage o'er?
  And is the star of genius fled?
And will his magic harp no more,
  Mute in the mansions of the dead,
Its strains seraphic pour?

A pilgrim in this world of woe,
  Condemn'd, alas! awhile to stray,
Where bristly thorns, where briers grow,
  He bade, to cheer the gloomy way,
Its heavenly music flow.

And oft he bade, by fame inspired,
  Its wild notes seek the ethereal plain,
Till angels, by its music fired,
  Have, listening, caught the ecstatic strain,
Have wonder'd, and admired.

But now secure on happier shores,
  With choirs of sainted souls he sings;
His harp the Omnipotent adores,
  And from its sweet, its silver strings
Celestial music pours.

And though on earth no more he'll weave
  The lay that's fraught with magic fire,
Yet oft shall Fancy hear at eve
  His now exalted heavenly lyre
In sounds Æolian grieve.

B. Stoke.

---

## SONNET IN MEMORY OF HENRY KIRKE WHITE.

BY J. G.

"'Tis now the dead of night," and I will go
To where the brook soft murmuring glides along
In the still wood; yet does the plaintive song
Of Philomela through the welkin flow;
And while pale Cynthia carelessly doth throw
  Her dewy beams the verdant boughs among,
  Will sit beneath some spreading oak tree strong,
And intermingle with the streams my woe!
Hush'd in deep silence every gentle breeze;
  No mortal breath disturbs the awful gloom;
Cold, chilling dewdrops trickle down the trees,
  And every flower withholds its rich perfume:
'Tis sorrow leads me to that sacred ground
Where Henry moulders in a sleep profound!

## LINES ON THE DEATH OF HENRY KIRKE WHITE.

LATE OF ST. JOHN'S COLLEGE, CAMBRIDGE.

Sorrows are mine — then let me joys evade,
And seek for sympathies in this lone shade.
The glooms of death fall heavy on my heart,
And, between life and me, a truce impart.
Genius has vanish'd in its opening bloom,
And youth and beauty wither in the tomb!
Thought, ever prompt to lend the inquiring eye,
Pursues thy spirit through futurity.
Does thy aspiring mind new powers essay,
Or in suspended being wait the day,
When earth shall fall before the awful train
Of Heaven and Virtue's everlasting reign?
May goodness, which thy heart did once enthrone,
Emit one ray to meliorate my own!
And for thy sake, when time affliction calm,
Science shall please, and poesie shall charm.
I turn my steps whence issued all my woes,
Where the dull courts monastic glooms impose;
Thence fled a spirit whose unbounded scope
Surpass'd the fond creations e'en of hope.
Along this path thy living step has fled,
Along this path they bore thee to the dead.

All that this languid eye can now survey
Witness'd the vigour of thy fleeting day:
And witness'd all, as speaks this anguish'd tear,
The solemn progress of thy early bier.
  Sacred the walls that took thy parting breath,
Own'd thee in life, encompass'd thee in death!
  Oh! I can feel as felt the sorrowing friend
Who o'er thy corse in agony did bend;
Dead as thyself to all the world inspires,
Paid the last rites mortality requires;
Closed the dim eye that beam'd with mind before.
Composed the icy limbs to move no more!
  Some power the picture from my memory tear,
Or feeling will rush onward to despair.
  Immortal hopes! come, lend your blest relief,
And raise the soul bow'd down with mortal grief;
Teach it to look for comfort in the skies:
Earth cannot give what Heaven's high will denies

Cambridge, Nov. 1806.

## SONNET

ADDRESSED TO H. K. WHITE, ON HIS POEMS LATELY PUBLISHED.

BY G. L. C.

Henry! I greet thine entrance into life!
Sure presage that the myrmidons of fate,
The fool's unmeaning laugh, the critic's hate,
Will dire assail thee; and the envious strife

Of bookish schoolmen, beings over rife,
Whose pia-mater studious is fill'd
With unconnected matter, half distill'd
From letter'd page, shall bare for thee the knife,
Beneath whose edge the poet ofttimes sinks:
But fear not! for thy modest work contains
The germ of worth; thy wild poetic strains,
How sweet to him, untutor'd bard, who thinks
Thy verse "has power to please, as soft it flows
Through the smooth murmurs of the frequent close."

1803.

## TO THE MEMORY OF HENRY KIRKE WHITE.

BY A LADY.

If worth, if genius, to the world are dear,
To Henry's shade devote no common tear;
His worth on no precarious tenure hung,
From genuine piety his virtues sprung;
If pure benevolence, if steady sense,
Can to the feeling heart delight dispense:
If all the highest efforts of the mind,
Exalted, noble, elegant, refined,
Call for fond sympathy's heart-felt regret,
Ye sons of genius, pay the mournful debt:
His friends can truly speak how large his claim,
And "Life was only wanting to his fame."

Art thou, indeed, dear youth, for ever fled?
So quickly number'd with the silent dead?
Too sure I read it in the downcast eye,
Hear it in mourning friendship's stifled sigh.
Ah! could esteem or admiration save
So dear an object from the untimely grave,
This transcript faint had not essay'd to tell
The loss of one beloved, revered so well;
Vainly I try, even eloquence were weak,
The silent sorrow that I feel to speak.
No more my hours of pain thy voice will cheer,
And bind my spirit to this lower sphere;
Bend o'er my suffering frame with gentle sigh,
And bid new fire relume my languid eye:
No more the pencil's mimic art command,
And with kind pity guide my trembling hand;
Nor dwell upon the page in fond regard,
To trace the meaning of the Tuscan bard.
Vain all the pleasures thou canst not inspire,
And "in my breast the imperfect joys expire."
I fondly hoped thy hand might grace my shrine,
And little dream'd I should have wept o'er thine:
In fancy's eye methought I saw thy lyre
With virtue's energies each bosom fire;
I saw admiring nations press around,
Eager to catch the animating sound:
And when, at length, sunk in the shades of night,
To brighter worlds thy spirit wing'd its flight,
Thy country hail'd thy venerated shade,
And each graced honour to thy memory paid.

Such was the fate hope pictured to my view —
But who, alas! e'er found hope's visions true?
And, ah! a dark presage, when last we met,
Sadden'd the social hour with deep regret;
When thou thy portrait from the minstrel drew,
The living Edwin starting on my view —
Silent, I ask'd of Heaven a lengthen'd date;
His genius thine, but not like thine his fate.
Shuddering I gazed, and saw too sure revealed,
The fatal truth, by hope till then conceal'd.
Too strong the portion of celestial flame
For its weak tenement the fragile frame;
Too soon for us it sought its native sky,
And soar'd impervious to the mortal eye,
Like some clear planet, shadow'd from our sight,
Leaving behind long tracks of lucid light:
So shall thy bright example fire each youth
With love of virtue, piety, and truth.
Long o'er thy loss shall grateful Granta mourn,
And bid her sons revere thy favour'd urn.
When thy loved flower "spring's victory makes known,"
The primrose pale shall bloom for thee alone:
Around thy urn the rosemary well spread,
Whose "tender fragrance," — emblem of the dead —
Shall "teach the maid, whose bloom no longer lives,"
That "virtue every perish'd grace survives."
Farewell! sweet Moralist; heart-sickening grief
Tells me in duty's path to seek relief,

With surer aim on faith's strong pinions rise,
And seek hope's vanish'd anchor in the skies.
Yet still on thee shall fond remembrance dwell,
And to the world thy worth delight to tell;
Though well I feel unworthy thee the lays
That to thy memory weeping friendship pays.

---

## STANZAS,

### SUPPOSED TO HAVE BEEN WRITTEN AT THE GRAVE OF HENRY KIRKE WHITE.

BY A LADY.

YE gentlest gales! oh, hither waft,
  On airy undulating sweeps,
Your frequent sighs so passing soft,
  Where he, the youthful Poet, sleeps!
He breathed the purest tenderest sigh,
The sigh of sensibility.

And thou shalt lie, his favourite flower,
  Pale primrose, on his grave reclined;
Sweet emblem of his fleeting hour,
  And of his pure, his spotless mind!
Like thee he sprung in lowly vale;
And felt, like thee, the trying gale.

Nor hence thy pensive eye seclude,
 O thou, the fragrant rosemary,
Where he, "in marble solitude,
 So peaceful and so deep" doth lie!
His harp prophetic sung to thee
In notes of sweetest minstrelsy.

Ye falling dews, Oh! ever leave
 Your crystal drops these flowers to steep:
At earliest morn, at latest eve,
 Oh let them for their poet weep!
For tears bedew'd his gentle eye,
The tears of heavenly sympathy.

Thou western Sun, effuse thy beams;
 For he was wont to pace the glade,
To watch in pale uncertain gleams,
 The crimson-zoned horizon fade—
Thy last, thy setting radiance pour,
Where he is set to rise no more.

THE END.

www.ingramcontent.com/pod-product-compliance
Lightning Source LLC
LaVergne TN
LVHW020223110826
845151LV00003B/806

* 9 7 8 1 4 2 5 5 3 2 5 9 8 *